MORNINGS WITH GOD for TEEN GIRLS

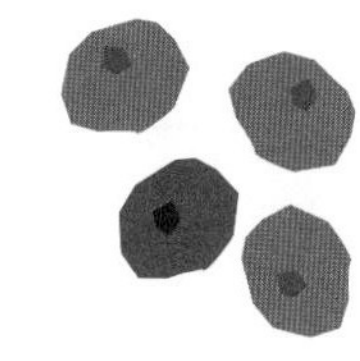

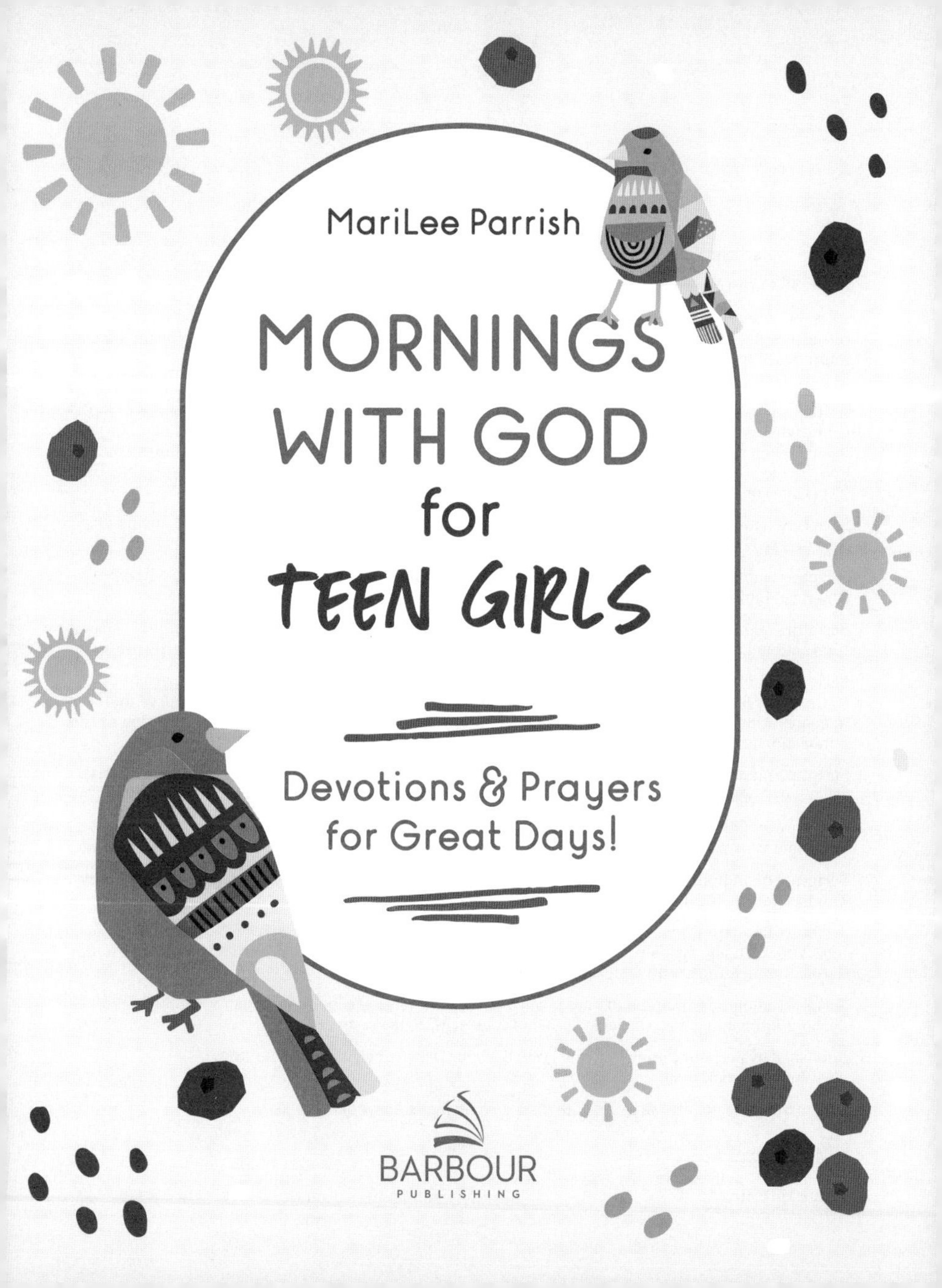
MariLee Parrish
MORNINGS
WITH GOD
for
TEEN GIRLS
Devotions & Prayers
for Great Days!
BARBOUR
PUBLISHING

Print ISBN 978-1-63609-616-2

Published by Barbour Publishing, Inc., 1810 Barbour Drive, Uhrichsville, Ohio 44683, www.barbourbooks.com

Our mission is to inspire the world with the life-changing message of the Bible.

Printed in China.

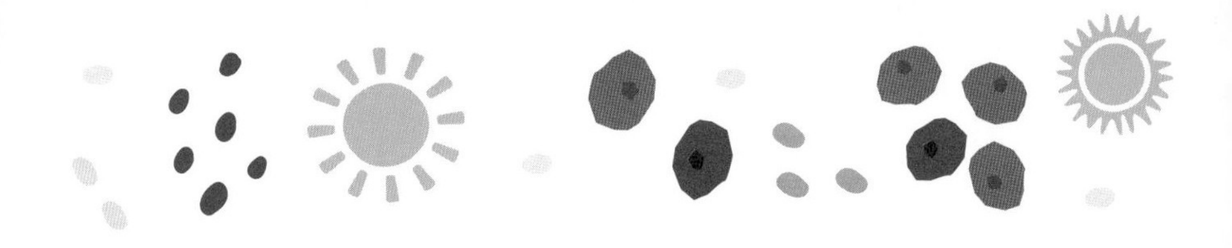

INTRODUCTION

O my soul, bless God! God, my God, how great you are! beautifully, gloriously robed, dressed up in sunshine.
Psalm 104:1–2 MSG

Good morning, girl! If you've opened this book, you're already well on your way to making this the *best day ever*!

Every page of this uplifting devotional will help you start your day right—in quiet time and conversation with the heavenly Father, the one who loves you most.

These 180 inspiring readings and prayers touch on topics important to your heart—positive thinking, confidence, joy, belonging, trust, hope, and so much more! With each turn of the page, you'll be gifted with a positive faith-building message guaranteed to start your day off right!

Be blessed!

YOU ARE LOVED!

We know and rely on the love God has for us. God is love. Whoever lives in love lives in God, and God in them.

1 John 4:16 NIV

To start any day off right, you have to know who you are. Or better yet, *whose* you are!

Here's what the Bible says:

- You are a beloved child of the Father (John 1:12; Galatians 4:6).
- You are loved with an everlasting love (Jeremiah 31:3).
- You are a new creation (2 Corinthians 5:17).
- You are righteous and holy (Ephesians 4:24).
- You are chosen, holy, and dearly loved (Colossians 3:12).
- God knows everything about you (Psalm 139).
- Nothing can separate you from God's love (Romans 8:38–39).
- Jesus calls you His friend (John 15:15).

That's your true identity as a follower of Jesus Christ! Start today by agreeing with God's truth about who you are. You are God's treasure! Remember this throughout your day.

If you haven't yet chosen to follow Jesus with your whole heart, make that choice today and write down the date so you can look back and see that today was the greatest day ever! It's the best choice you'll ever make.

Jesus, I choose to follow You. I believe You paid the price for all my sin on the cross. Come into my heart and change me by the power of Your Holy Spirit.

FLIP THE SWITCH

We are taking every thought and purpose captive to the obedience of Christ.
2 CORINTHIANS 10:5 AMP

Good morning, friend! Let's start this day by talking about something really important. You have a choice to make every day when you wake up: Will you see everything that happens through your physical eyes or through eyes of faith?

Without faith, doubt and fear can creep in and start controlling your thoughts and actions. Then the unbelieving culture we live in will start to matter more than it should. Jesus wants to show you another way. He wants to help you flip the switch in your brain to see things His way, through eyes of faith. And you never have to try to figure that out on your own. Jesus simply says, "Come to me." And He will help you learn how "to live freely and lightly" (Matthew 11:28–30 MSG).

As you flip your light switch on to start your day, let that be a reminder to allow your thoughts to come under the power of the Holy Spirit. Ask Him to guide you throughout your day. Say Jesus' name in your mind or out loud when you're struggling with your thoughts or feeling down. Let Him help.

Lord, please flip the switch in my brain to see things through Your eyes today.

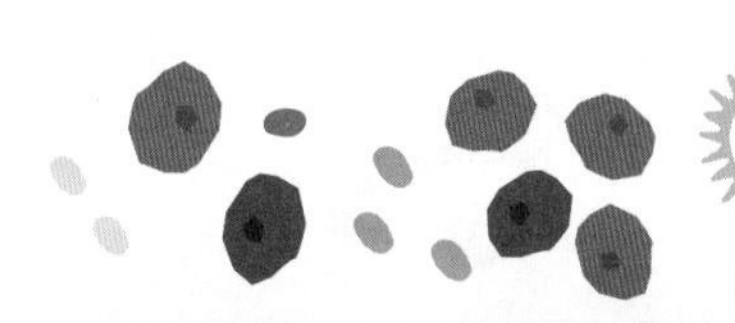

SIMPLY JESUS

Do not conform to the pattern of this world, but be transformed by the renewing of your mind. Then you will be able to test and approve what God's will is—his good, pleasing and perfect will.

Romans 12:2 niv

So how did it go yesterday? Were you able to see things through eyes of faith a little better? If so, hooray! Celebrate that today and keep doing what you're doing!

If you still struggled with your thoughts, know that you're not alone. We all have times of doubt. Learning to "take captive every thought" (2 Corinthians 10:5) and make it subject to Jesus is a lifelong learning process. No one gets everything right all the time. Nobody's perfect. No one except Jesus, that is. And it turns out that He's the one with the power to help!

Jesus really does want to help you transform your thoughts and to seek and see Him in all things. Today, say His name over your life. Write a sticky note or place a reminder somewhere that simply says "Jesus." Drawing your mind back to the one who knows you best and loves you most can change your day.

Lord Jesus, thank You for loving me and wanting the best for me. I give You permission to transform my heart and mind. I want to know Your will and follow You all the days of my life.

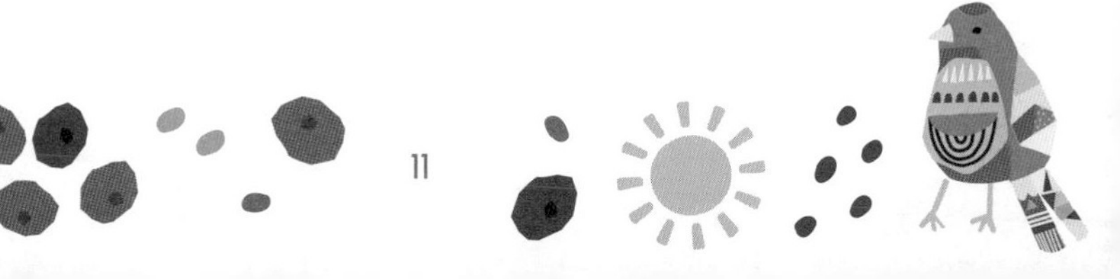

STARTING OUT RIGHT

Finally, brothers and sisters, whatever is true, whatever is noble, whatever is right, whatever is pure, whatever is lovely, whatever is admirable—if anything is excellent or praiseworthy—think about such things.

PHILIPPIANS 4:8 NIV

Start this day with good things on your mind. Take a minute to thank God for all He's done for you. Even if you're going through a rough time, you have so much to be thankful for. Think back to all the ways God has cared for you throughout your lifetime. Have you seen His hand guiding you in certain ways? What are you most thankful for in your life right now?

Make a habit of writing down the ways you've seen God work in your life. That way, if you are tempted to doubt or struggle with wondering if God is there, you can have a black-and-white reminder that He is—and always has been—at work in your life.

Beginning each day with thankfulness can set the tone for everything else that happens. Yep, you may face some hard things today. Jesus said there would be trouble in this world. But He also said to "take heart" because He's overcome it (John 16:33). And He can help you overcome it too.

Good morning, Lord. I'm thankful for the gift of this day! Thanks for being with me always.

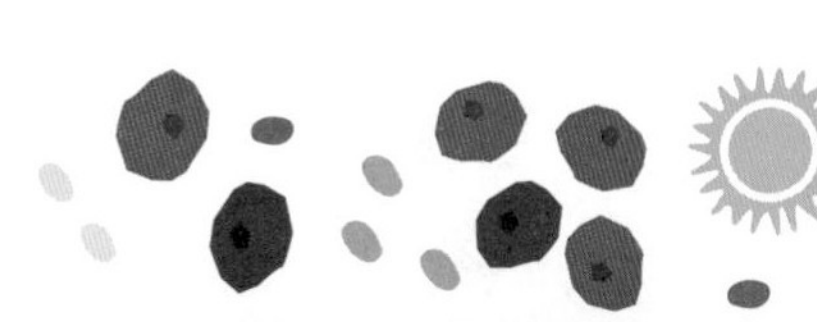

GOODBYE, ANXIETY

Do not be anxious about anything, but in every situation, by prayer and petition, with thanksgiving, present your requests to God. And the peace of God, which transcends all understanding, will guard your hearts and your minds in Christ Jesus.

PHILIPPIANS 4:6–7 NIV

When's the last time you felt your stomach tie up in knots over something that was going on in your life? That's what anxiety feels like. When your brain gets a signal that you are upset and anxious about something, it makes physical changes to your body. Frequent stress and anxiety can be very hard on your body and can cause you to get sick.

God has good plans for your life, and He wants you to know some important things about anxiety. Instead of being stressed, anxious, and worried about things, He wants you to bring all of those thoughts and feelings to Him! And guess what He says will happen when you do that? He'll give you His peace to guard your heart and mind.

Can you try that right now? What has you worried, girl? Bring that to Jesus. Picture yourself carrying all of these heavy loads to Jesus and laying them down. What does He want you to know about the things you're stressed about?

Jesus, I don't want to be anxious today.
Will You show me how to let go of these worries?

IT'S A GOOD DAY

"You will keep in perfect and constant peace the one whose mind is steadfast [that is, committed and focused on You—in both inclination and character], because he trusts and takes refuge in You [with hope and confident expectation]."

ISAIAH 26:3 AMP

Today's gonna be a good day. Why? Because God is with you. He promises never to leave you. Check it out:

- "Be strong and courageous. Do not fear or be in dread of them, for it is the LORD your God who goes with you. He will not leave you or forsake you." (Deuteronomy 31:6 ESV)
- "So do not fear, for I am with you." (Isaiah 41:10 NIV)
- "Surely I am with you always, to the very end of the age." (Matthew 28:20 NIV)
- "Never will I leave you; never will I forsake you." (Hebrews 13:5 NIV)

These are good verses to memorize and keep close to your heart and mind. Isaiah tells us that God keeps us in His perfect peace when our minds are focused on God and committed to Him. That doesn't mean that nothing bad is going to happen; it means that God is with you in all things and is always available to provide miraculous and creative solutions to everything you face.

Lord, I believe it's going to be a good day because You're with me in all things!

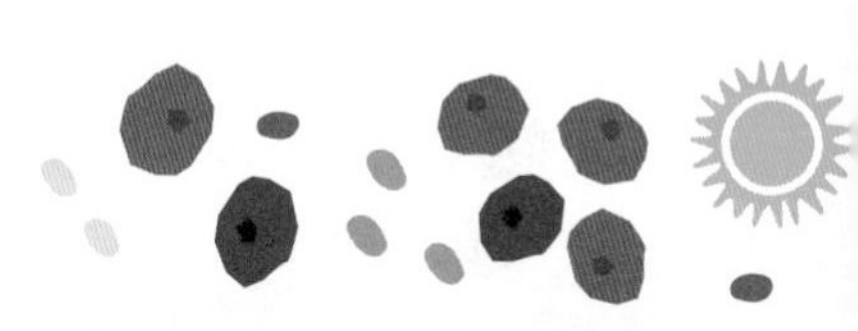

GUARD YOUR THOUGHTS

Above all else, guard your heart, for everything you do flows from it.
PROVERBS 4:23 NIV

The book of Proverbs is full of wise words to live by. Today's verse reminds us to guard our hearts. The Easy-to-Read version of this verse says, "Above all, be careful what you think because your thoughts control your life."

Your thoughts and feelings aren't always truth. Read that again.

Just because you feel something and might even really, really, really think it *is* true, doesn't mean it is. Take Jen, for instance. She was a beautiful, tall girl who brightened every room. But a mean-spirited boy told her she was fat when she was in middle school, and she took his words to heart. No matter what anyone else said, even the doctor who declared her healthy, she believed a lie. And it changed the way she acted around others for most of her life.

Your thoughts matter. Commit today to think only the thoughts that are true from God's Word. You are His beautiful daughter. Created for a purpose. Blessed beyond measure. A princess in God's kingdom.

When dark thoughts that bring you down come into your mind, command them to leave in Jesus' name and replace them with truth from His Word.

Wow, Lord. I'm beginning to see that the things I think about are really important to You. Help me think Your thoughts, Jesus.

INVITE JESUS IN

For such a person ought not to think or expect that he will receive anything [at all] from the Lord, being a double-minded man, unstable and restless in all his ways [in everything he thinks, feels, or decides].

JAMES 1:7–8 AMP

Have you ever felt so confused that you were stuck? You could not decide because there were so many options? Maybe your mind kept spinning so much that you could hardly even sleep. This happens to many people, especially when Jesus is left out of the equation.

First Corinthians 14:33 (ESV) says, "God is not a God of confusion but of peace."

The next time you have a big decision to make, take it to Jesus. Imagine all of the scenarios, but invite Jesus in. Ask Him to show you the next step. Picture Him in your mind, helping you make the decision and imagining the outcome. Sit in the quiet with Him and ask what He would like you to know.

God created your imagination, and He wants to speak to you in countless ways. If you're not sure that something you've heard is from God, ask Him to confirm it. When God shows you something in your mind, it will always line up with the truth in His Word.

Lord Jesus, let Your Spirit rise up in me and lead me into Your truth.

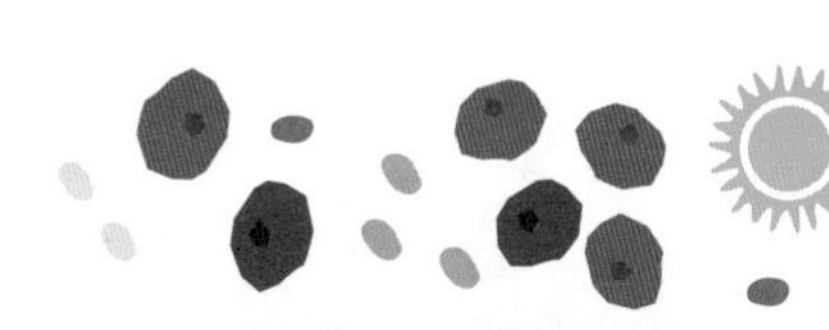

A NEW SET OF CLOTHES

You were taught, with regard to your former way of life, to put off your old self, which is being corrupted by its deceitful desires; to be made new in the attitude of your minds; and to put on the new self, created to be like God in true righteousness and holiness.

EPHESIANS 4:22–24 NIV

Isn't it fun to get a bunch of new clothes? There's nothing quite like wearing a new outfit for the first time. Ephesians 4 talks about putting on something new too. When Jesus came into your heart, the old and dirty stuff got tossed away for good, and Jesus covered you in something brand-new: His robe of righteousness.

Isaiah 61:10 (AMP) says, "I will rejoice greatly in the LORD, my soul will exult in my God; for He has clothed me with garments of salvation, He has covered me with a robe of righteousness." This is a great verse to write out on a sticky note and hang on your mirror!

When you get dressed this morning, picture yourself putting on the robe of Christ's righteousness. This is who you were created to be!

Jesus, I'm thankful that You've taken away all the old and dirty stuff in my life. You've made my heart brand-new, and I'm covered in Your royal robes. Please remind me of this all throughout this day.

PRAYING GOD'S WILL

"Father, if you are willing, take this cup from me; yet not my will, but yours be done."

LUKE 22:42 NIV

Have you ever wanted something so badly that you couldn't think of anything else? Maybe it was getting the lead part in the school play or something serious like wanting a family member to heal from an illness. Jesus showed us what to do with our wants in Luke 22. He was telling His Father how He really felt—bringing all His thoughts and feelings to His Father and pouring His heart out.

Jesus asked His Father for what He wanted, but then He laid down His request in surrender. He said, "Yet not my will, but yours be done."

Have you laid down your wants in surrender to God's will? He may very well want you to have the lead in the school play so that you can bring glory and honor to Him. Or He may have something entirely different in mind for you because He loves you and He can see all ends. Whatever your wants, you can trust God to do what's best for you.

Tell God what's on your heart. And then lay it down. His will for you is always the best.

Jesus, I want to be more like You. Help me surrender my wants for Your perfect will.

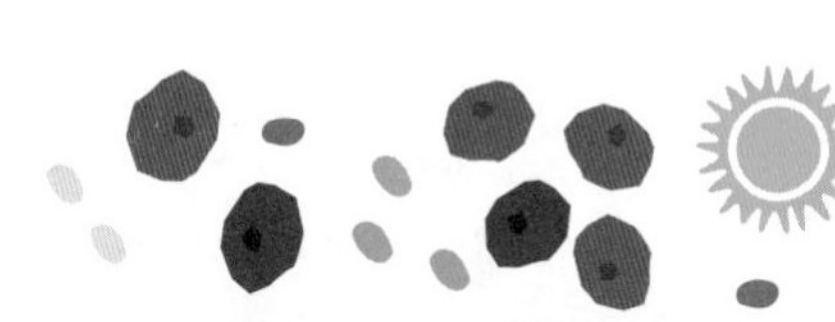

WHAT'S INSIDE YOUR HEART?

"Whatever comes from the mouth has come out of the heart. These things make the man unclean inside."
MATTHEW 15:18 NLV

Do you ever stop to listen to yourself talk? That might seem funny, but what you hear yourself saying to the people closest to you is generally what you really think in your heart and mind.

Most people expose their hearts and their true selves to the safe people around them. What do you find yourself saying to the people who live in your house? Stop and listen. Yeah, your family might think you're extra crazy when you stop talking midsentence, but why not add a little comedic mystery to your family life and find out what's inside your heart?

If you hear yourself saying whatever comes to mind without first thinking about how your words might affect the people you love, it's time to do something about that. Ask the Holy Spirit to help you with this. Start your morning by surrendering your heart and your words to Jesus.

Jesus, I know my words are important to You because they reveal what's in my heart. I surrender my words and my heart to You today. Please help me speak out of the love You are growing in my heart.

THE BUBBLE

Set your mind and keep focused habitually on the things above [the heavenly things], not on things that are on the earth [which have only temporal value].
COLOSSIANS 3:2 AMP

When I was in high school, it seemed like nothing else existed. Our little school in our little town was the center of the universe. I didn't really care what was happening anywhere else in the world because the people I saw every day at school were the only ones who mattered to me. It was my bubble. My choices were directly influenced by those people, from what clothes I chose to wear to school to how I thought about myself. My mind was focused on earthly things.

One summer I went on a mission trip, and that bubble began to pop. I could suddenly see outside of my own little world, and my thinking changed in lots of ways.

Do you find yourself in a bubble sometimes? Talk to Jesus about this. Ask Him to expand your thoughts in heavenly ways. Ask Him to give you His vision for your life and your world.

Lord, I don't want to get stuck in a bubble. Help me to think Your way. Please give me eyes to see You at work in the world. Show me how I can be a part of what You're doing.

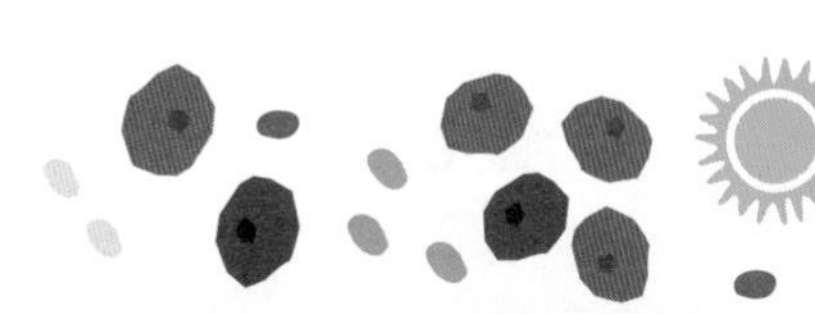

START YOUR DAY WITH JESUS

"Call to Me and I will answer you, and tell you [and even show you] great and mighty things, [things which have been confined and hidden], which you do not know and understand and cannot distinguish."

JEREMIAH 33:3 AMP

What do you think about when you first wake up? What you have going on today? What you're going to wear? Breakfast? I mean, it has been a long time since dinner, right? A girl has to eat! All those things are normal to think about when waking. But what would it look like to wake up with Jesus on your mind?

Jesus is with you always. He promised you that. And He always keeps His promises. He's there. Smiling as you blink your eyes open and yawn. One foot on the floor and then another. He sees you. Instead of rushing off to start your day, try practicing thankfulness as you wake. Thank God for being there. He wants you to call to Him and listen for His voice in your life.

Write today's verse on a note card, and place it on your nightstand so that you'll see it first thing every morning. Starting your day with Jesus can make all the difference!

Jesus, thanks for being with me. I love You. I'm thankful that You want to speak to me.

FOCUS ON HOPE

I would have despaired had I not believed that I would see the goodness of the Lord in the land of the living.

Psalm 27:13 AMP

There was a time when I was sick for months and months. It took a lot of tests and various medical professionals to figure out the cause. During that time, I chewed on these words daily in Acts 2:25–28 (NIV): "I saw the Lord always before me. Because he is at my right hand, I will not be shaken. Therefore my heart is glad and my tongue rejoices; my body also will rest in hope, because you will not abandon me to the realm of the dead, you will not let your holy one see decay. You have made known to me the paths of life; you will fill me with joy in your presence."

These words gave me hope every day. I chose to focus on them instead of on the pain in my body. And even though I was hurting, Jesus gave me joy on the inside because I knew He was with me. It would have been easy to give in to depression and despair during that difficult time, but Jesus was close.

Jesus, thank You for Your amazing promises. You really do fill me with joy and hope as I spend time in Your presence, no matter the circumstances.

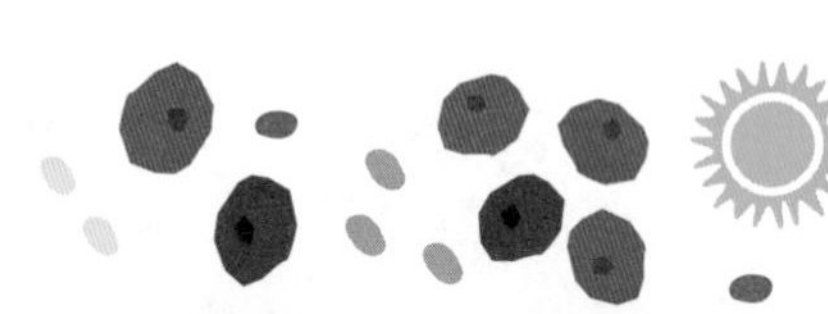

ANXIOUS THOUGHTS

Search me, O God, and know my heart; test me and know my anxious thoughts. Point out anything in me that offends you, and lead me along the path of everlasting life.

Psalm 139:23–24 NLT

It's so easy to become anxious these days. If you spend any amount of time on social media, you're likely to be anxious in minutes. Psalm 139 has a good solution for this! Ask God to search you and point out anything that is getting in the way of your relationship with Him. He knows your heart, and He wants to lead you on your journey moment by moment.

If you find yourself feeling anxious, turn off the screen and get alone with God. Talk to Him. Share your heart and feelings with Him.

While everyone you know may be spending more and more time online, ask Jesus if that's what He wants for you. He has special plans and purposes for your life. Having good boundaries online and setting limits for yourself can help prevent anxiety and keep you focused on all the good things God has for you. Start your day with Jesus instead of social media and notice how your anxiety decreases!

Jesus, help me to have good boundaries online. I bring my anxious thoughts to You. Please reveal anything that's getting in the way of You speaking to me.

WAKIN' UP GRUMPY

Why am I discouraged? Why is my heart so sad? I will put my hope in God! I will praise him again—my Savior and my God! Now I am deeply discouraged, but I will remember you.
PSALM 42:5–6 NLT

We all wake up feeling down sometimes. Allergies, physical illness, or not getting enough sleep the night before can make crawling out of bed feel like a difficult chore. But even on those days when you wake up grumpy, God is with you. It's important to know that feelings aren't necessarily bad. God gave us the ability to feel for a reason. But not all feelings are truth.

A good habit to get into is to take all your thoughts and feelings to Jesus. He doesn't want you to hide how you truly feel. He wants to help you express those feelings in a safe place—with Him! And He'll help you align those feelings with truth from His Word.

So if you wake up grumpy, there's no need to paste on a fake smile and pretend. First, take your feelings to Jesus and let Him help. Talk to Him before you do anything else.

Lord, I'm not feeling too great today. I bring all these thoughts and feelings to You. Please help me sort them out. Help me live by the truth of who You say I am instead of how I feel today.

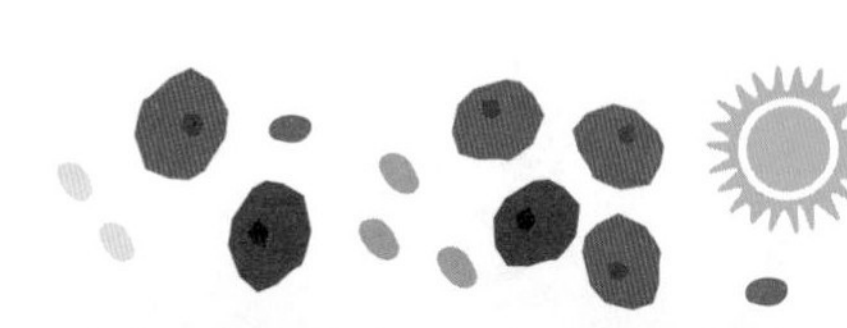

CHRIST'S SPIRIT

Spiritually alive, we have access to everything God's Spirit is doing, and can't be judged by unspiritual critics. Isaiah's question, "Is there anyone around who knows God's Spirit, anyone who knows what he is doing?" has been answered: Christ knows, and we have Christ's Spirit.

1 Corinthians 2:14–16 MSG

Abby was a sweet and kind teenager. She had a lot of talent, and she loved people. The problem was that she was scared to offend anyone. She worried a lot about what other people thought of her, and so she tried to please everyone. She was devastated when anyone criticized her. But that's not what God wanted for Abby. He gave her gifts and talents to point others to Jesus. And when she let the words of others (even "unspiritual critics" who didn't even know Jesus) penetrate her heart and mind, her relationship with Jesus suffered.

If you are a follower of Jesus, you have His Spirit alive and at work in you right now. Allow His voice to be the loudest one you hear and the one you allow to seep deeply into your heart and mind.

Lord Jesus, I'm thankful for Your Spirit who is working in my heart! Please help me not to worry about what other people think of me and to live my life to follow You instead.

LIFE AND PEACE

I've tried everything and nothing helps. I'm at the end of my rope. Is there no one who can do anything for me? . . . The answer, thank God, is that Jesus Christ can and does. He acted to set things right in this life of contradictions where I want to serve God with all my heart and mind, but am pulled by the influence of sin to do something totally different.

Romans 7:24–25 msg

Can you relate to this scripture at all? You try to think good thoughts, but you struggle. You confess the same sin over and over. You want to make the right choice, but you fail.

Many people run away from God when they can't get a handle on their sin. But that's the exact opposite of what needs to happen. Romans 8:1 (NLT) promises, "So now there is no condemnation for those who belong to Christ Jesus."

Run back to Jesus every time you fail. You will find His grace. The Spirit of God is alive in you, bringing life and peace instead of sin and death (see Romans 8:6).

Lord, I'm struggling with my thoughts again, and I'm running to You. I know that I'm covered in Your righteousness and that is the only reason I can come to You confidently. Please fill me with Your truth and peace.

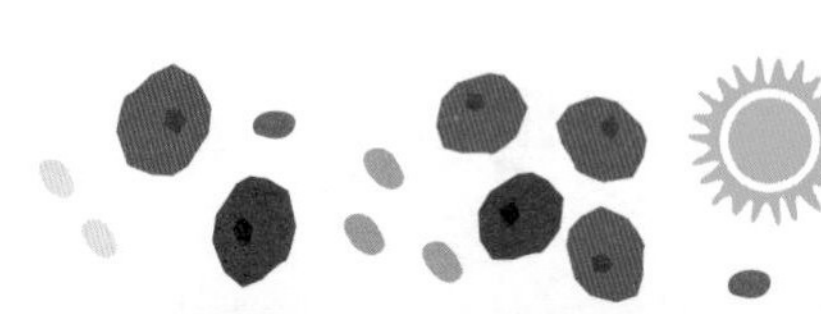

THE WAR

But there is another power within me that is at war with my mind.
ROMANS 7:23 NLT

The Bible tells us that we're in the middle of a war between good and evil. A spiritual battle is being waged all around you even though you can't see it with your physical eyes.

Have you ever seen your actual heart? The one that beats inside your body? Probably not. But you know it's there or you would be dead, right? Just like that, there is a battle going on all around you.

You have an enemy. Jesus calls him the "father of lies" (John 8:44). Satan's goal is to steal, kill, and destroy. But you are a warrior princess! Take courage because you are not alone in the fight. John 10:10 (NLT) says this: "The thief's purpose is to steal and kill and destroy. My purpose is to give them a rich and satisfying life."

Does God want you to fear the battle? Nope. He wants you to be prepared and ready to fight when the time is right. You can be confident because He has given you weapons and armor to protect you (see Ephesians 6:10–18).

Lord, I put on the full armor of God today. I won't fear the battle because You are with me, bringing strength, confidence, and protection.

NO MORE LIES

The Spirit God gave us does not make us timid,
but gives us power, love and self-discipline.
2 TIMOTHY 1:7 NIV

Kayla, a teenage girl who had a rough childhood, was struggling with fear. The enemy kept telling her lies about her worth, and she was beginning to believe them. She didn't know much about who God said she was, so she fell for the lies she was hearing in her mind.

God knew that Kayla was struggling, and He worked in amazing ways to get her attention. She gave her life to Jesus, and she learned about 2 Timothy 1:7. The version she memorized was this: "God has not given us a spirit of fear, but of power and of love and of a sound mind" (NKJV).

That "sound mind" part really stuck with her. To her, it meant that she was smart, capable, and not crazy! Whenever those old lies tried to sneak in and take over her mind, she would quickly recall 2 Timothy 1:7. She would even say it out loud, since many times those lies came to her mind when she was alone in her car. Now she's able to recognize what's happening and tell herself the truth from God's Word!

Lord, thank You for giving me truth to
counter the lies that come at me!

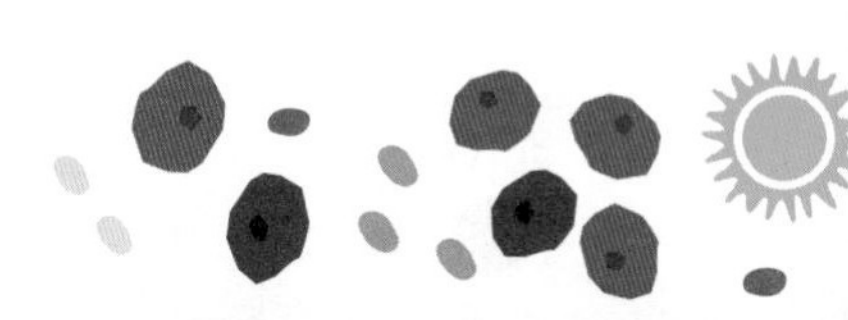

QUICK JUDGMENT

"The Lord does not look at the things people look at. People look at the outward appearance, but the Lord looks at the heart."
1 Samuel 16:7 niv

Have you ever looked at someone new and had a quick judgment about them in your heart? Maybe you were at the grocery store and saw someone quite different from you, and your first thought was something negative about that person. When that happens, don't let that thought linger. Get in the habit of quickly taking that thought straight to Jesus and confessing it. Ask Him to forgive you for judging others by their appearance. And then begin to pray a blessing over that person you thought negatively about. Pray that they would come to know the love of Jesus if they don't already know Him.

As you know, what you think determines what you do next. If you are praying blessings over a person, it will be so much easier to reach out and say a kind word to them. But if you are judging them in your mind, it will be nearly impossible to reach out in love.

Lord, I confess that I often judge others by what they look like or what they're doing, and I'm sorry for that. Please change my heart and mind to see others the way You see them.

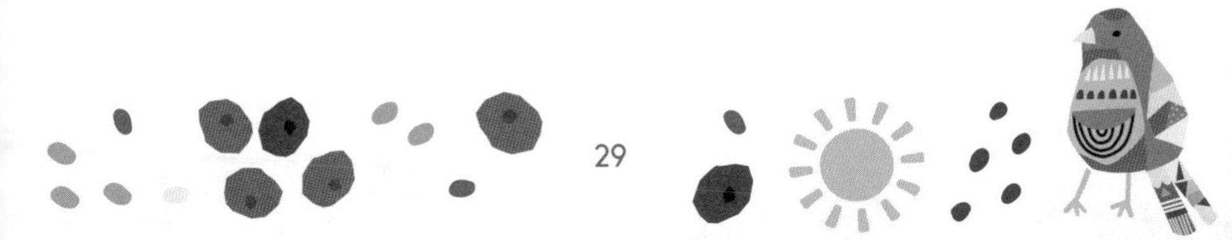

LOVING GOD

Jesus replied: "'Love the Lord your God with all your heart and with all your soul and with all your mind.'"
MATTHEW 22:37 NIV

Check out *The Message* paraphrase of this verse: "Jesus said, 'Love the Lord your God with all your passion and prayer and intelligence.' This is the most important, the first on any list." That's an interesting way to look at it, right? If passion is defined as "powerful feelings," what would happen if you directed all of those powerful feelings at God? Do your prayers express your love for God? Is your intelligence dedicated to the love of God?

As you go throughout your day today, ask God to show you how you can love Him more with your heart, soul, strength, and mind. You may be amazed at all the ways God answers this question for you. Maybe He will answer through songs, through other people, or through a Bible verse the Holy Spirit brings to your mind, like this one: "If you love me, keep my commands. And I will ask the Father, and he will give you another advocate to help you and be with you forever—the Spirit of truth" (John 14:15–17 NIV).

Lord, I want to learn how to love You with all of my thoughts and feelings. I want to think thoughts that show my love and honor for You.

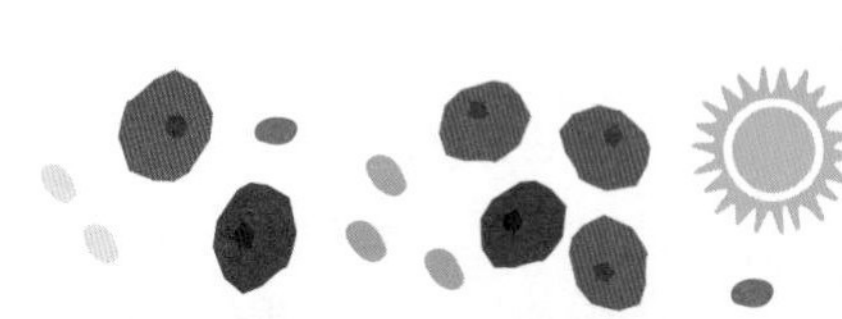

BE INTENTIONAL

So prepare your minds for action, be completely sober [in spirit—steadfast, self-disciplined, spiritually and morally alert], fix your hope completely on the grace [of God] that is coming to you when Jesus Christ is revealed.

1 PETER 1:13 AMP

What's your plan for today? Have you checked your schedule? Whether it's school, chores, friends, or family, there are days when you know you have to show up and be prepared. If it's test day, you have to study. If it's a coffee date with friends at the café, you have to have some money.

As a follower of Jesus, it's important to be intentional too. Every moment is an opportunity to trust God and bring His life and love to those around you.

The Message paraphrase concludes this paragraph in 1 Peter 1:14–16 by saying, "As obedient children, let yourselves be pulled into a way of life shaped by God's life, a life energetic and blazing with holiness. God said, 'I am holy; you be holy.'"

Allow your life to be shaped by God's life every single day. Be intentional about that. Why not start today?

Lord, it's probably going to be a busy day. I want to be intentional about bringing Your life and love to the people I'm with today. Would You please prompt me to do that at the right time?

GO TO THE SOURCE

I look up to the mountains—does my help come from there? My help comes from the LORD, who made heaven and earth!
PSALM 121:1–2 NLT

The writer of this psalm probably didn't mean for it to be humorous, but can you picture someone yelling at the mountains to help them with their problem?

Hellooo! I need some help!

Or maybe they're yelling at the people on the mountain?

Hey, you up there! I have a big problem! Can anyone help?

But the one who can actually take care of their problem is the Creator of those mountains Himself!

How often have you done this? You need some help and you ask Google, a friend, a hairstylist, a nurse, a doctor, a parent, a teacher. Asking for help in those places isn't necessarily a bad thing (well, the jury is still out on Google)—asking for help when you need it is a good thing! Just don't forget to go to the source first!

God cares about what you care about. If it's on your heart and mind, big or small, go to Jesus about it. He is Lord of all.

Lord, I'm sorry when I forget to come to You first. Teach me to trust that my help comes from You.

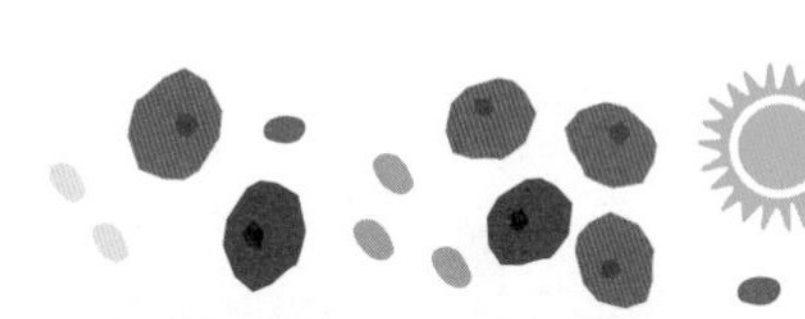

A GOOD LAUGH

A happy heart is good medicine and a joyful mind causes healing, but a broken spirit dries up the bones.

PROVERBS 17:22 AMP

What's your all-time favorite joke? Tell it to someone today!

You've probably heard it said that laughter is the best medicine. But did you know that there is actually scientific proof to back that up? Many studies show that when you laugh, your immune system is boosted, stress hormones and pain decrease, and those "feel-good" receptors increase. God created your body to work that way! And that right there is pretty amazing.

If you're struggling with hard things, maybe what you need is a good game night with some joyful people. Invite family and friends over and laugh your worries away. Being around other joyful people is healing in many ways too. The body of Christ is meant to carry one another's burdens and rejoice with one another. When we come together to enjoy life in God-honoring ways, good things happen to our hearts, minds, and bodies.

Tell some good jokes. Be silly with a friend. Take some time to thank God for the gift of laughter. You'll feel better.

Lord God, thanks for creating laughter. And thanks for creating my amazing body the way You did. Thanks also for friends and jokes that help me feel better.

100 PERCENT RIGHT

A person may think their own ways are right,
but the Lord weighs the heart.
Proverbs 21:2 NIV

I won't mention any names here (because he lives in our house and might become suspicious), but a teenage boy whom I know very well was in the habit of saying he was 100 percent sure of something. Turns out, in his mind, that left a little bit of margin for error. Soon he started saying 110 percent sure and then finally 150 percent sure. He needed a math refresher for sure! But how often do all of us do this?

We think we're right. Really, really right. Tell-everyone-who-will-listen right. But then. . .oops! Turns out, we were wrong.

Humility is the name of the game. Only God knows everything, including what's in our hearts. We can be really sure about something and still be really wrong.

Proverbs 11:2 (ESV) says, "When pride comes, then comes disgrace, but with the humble is wisdom."

Ask Jesus to help you have humble thoughts. Putting God first and being teachable and willing to admit your mistakes is being 100 percent right.

Lord Jesus, please help me have wisdom and humility. I don't need to be right all the time. Help me to be humble and loving.

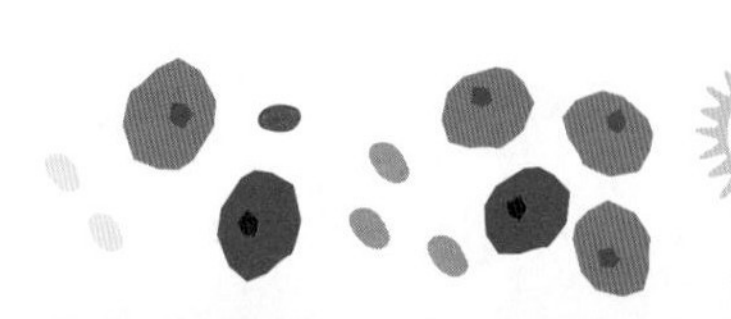

FEELINGS FOR PRESIDENT?

"Then you will know the truth, and the truth will set you free."
JOHN 8:32 NIV

Many schools have a student leaders program. Students are chosen because of leadership abilities, responsibility, maturity, and good grades. Good leaders show integrity, and that makes following them a good thing. But here's one you should definitely think twice about following: your feelings. Feelings are bad student leaders. Feelings try to make us follow them, but it should be the other way around! Remember, sometimes feelings don't reflect the truth.

Feelings might tell you that you're alone, incapable, dumb, unworthy, and on and on. None of those feelings should be followed.

Tell your feelings the truth today.

Repeat after me:

- I am loved and cherished.
- I am a child of the Most High God.
- I have been created for a purpose.
- God has good plans for my life.

These are truths from God's Word that you can believe in. The next time your feelings try to run for student president of your body, tell them to sit back down as you move forward in God's truth and purpose for your life.

Lord, I want to be wise when it comes to my feelings. Sometimes they can help inform me, but other times they aren't true. Help me learn the difference as I follow Your truth for my life.

LIFE OR DEATH

A man is tempted to do wrong when he lets himself be led by what his bad thoughts tell him to do. When he does what his bad thoughts tell him to do, he sins. When sin completes its work, it brings death.

JAMES 1:14–15 NLV

Today's scripture describes in detail what happens when we let feelings and bad thoughts lead. Sounds like a "choose your own adventure" that ends in death, doesn't it? Check it out:

1. A person is tempted (man is used here to depict all "mankind") by following his or her bad thoughts.
2. She sins because she let her bad thoughts tell her what to do.
3. Lots of natural consequences and bad things happen after giving in to bad thoughts and feelings.
4. Death is the end result of a life of sin.

Sounds pretty serious, right? It is! Your thoughts and feelings are a really big deal. That's why it's so important to learn how to control them when you're young and lead them by the power of the Holy Spirit alive in you!

Choose your own adventure by tapping into God's truth every day, and you'll live a full and abundant life (John 10:10)!

Lord, I want to choose a great adventure with You! One that leads to life. Help me learn how to control my thoughts and tell my feelings the truth by Your power.

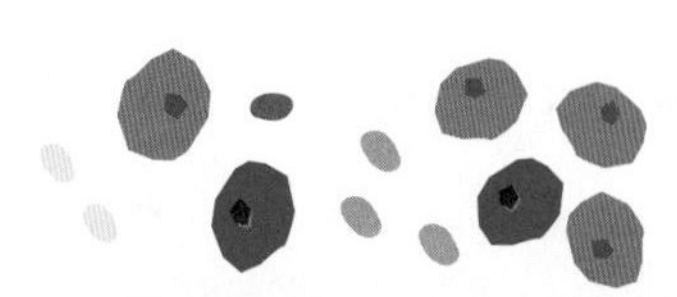

ENCOURAGE SOMEONE TODAY

Let us hold tightly without wavering to the hope we affirm, for God can be trusted to keep his promise.
HEBREWS 10:23 NLT

The writer of the book of Hebrews encouraged his readers to hold tight to their faith, to keep meeting together, and to encourage one another. In this world, it's easy to get discouraged and down. That's one of the reasons we need the body of Christ. We can lift one another up and "spur one another on toward love and good deeds" (Hebrews 10:24 NIV).

Who can you encourage today? Take a moment to make a list of the people you might run into today—a teacher, friends, parents, siblings, maybe the lady who does your hair. Think through your day and write down some names. Pray through your list. Ask God to give you a special encouragement for each of them today. Maybe a kind word or a simple hello and a big smile can make the difference in someone's life today.

In this world that is always telling them the opposite, remind someone that God is good and He can be trusted! Be an encourager today!

Lord Jesus, bring people to my mind today whom I can encourage. Help me share Your love and faithfulness with them.

TRUST OUR AMAZING GOD

Trust in the LORD with all your heart and lean not on your own understanding; in all your ways submit to him, and he will make your paths straight.

PROVERBS 3:5–6 NIV

Recently, a Christian counselor shared with me a true story of God healing a college student who had a misshapen foot. A group of young men were reading the scriptures together and came across some verses about God being able to heal. This young man had never even considered asking God to heal his foot. It had been that way since birth! But if the Bible is true, then God can do anything He wants to. And the things He's done before, He can still do if He chooses. So the young men prayed together, asking for healing, and watched in awe as the malformed foot was untwisted and completely healed!

The Bible is full of true miracle stories like that. That's the God we know, love, and serve. You can trust Him with your whole heart and lean on Him for understanding instead of trusting in yourself. Make room in your thoughts for God to amaze you with His wisdom and power.

Father, You are awesome and powerful.
Thank You for loving and leading me.

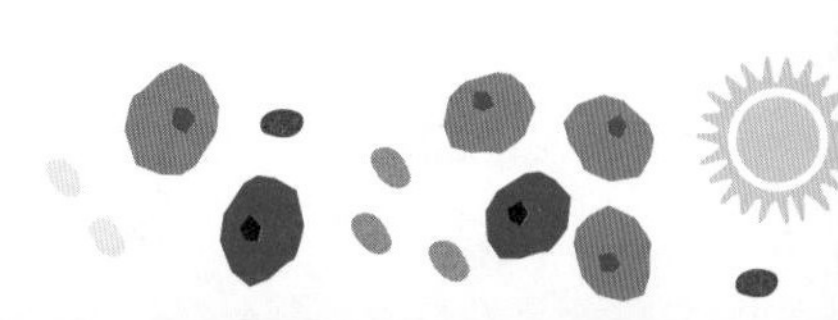

MY THOUGHTS ARE A BIG DEAL

Think as Christ Jesus thought.
PHILIPPIANS 2:5 NLV

Tomorrow we're going to start talking about confidence. But for today, let's recap what we've learned about our thoughts. Our thoughts are a big deal. Does God care what we think about? Yes, He absolutely does. How do we know? His Word tells us.

Here are some other scriptures that talk about our thoughts:

- "So letting your sinful nature control your mind leads to death. But letting the Spirit control your mind leads to life and peace." (Romans 8:6 NLT)
- "Let my words and my thoughts be pleasing to you, LORD, because you are my mighty rock and my protector." (Psalm 19:14 CEV)
- "Evil plans and thoughts of the wicked are exceedingly vile and offensive to the LORD, but pure words are pleasant words to Him." (Proverbs 15:26 AMP)
- "Commit your works to the LORD, and your thoughts will be established." (Proverbs 16:3 NKJV)

Lord Jesus, I think I'm starting to get it. I'm understanding that what I do with my thoughts and feelings is very important to You. I don't want to stew on thoughts and feelings that aren't truth. I commit my mind and my heart to You. When stray thoughts and bad feelings come into my head, nudge me, Lord. Remind me that You're there and that I can bring everything to You.

CONFIDENCE

So do not throw away your confidence; it will be richly rewarded. You need to persevere so that when you have done the will of God, you will receive what he has promised.
HEBREWS 10:35–36 NIV

Dictionary.com defines confidence like this: "1. full trust; belief in the powers, trustworthiness, or reliability of a person or thing. 2. belief in oneself and one's powers or abilities; self-confidence; self-reliance; assurance."

Which definition do you think the Bible is talking about? Let's try out this sentence: "So do not throw away your belief in yourself and your own powers and abilities." Nope. Doesn't work. That sounds like the world talking to you, or maybe a superhero convention, and not the Bible.

God wants you to hang tight to your confidence in *Him*. In His powers. In His trustworthiness. In His reliability and faithfulness. Humans can never meet all those demands. And if your trust is in yourself, you'll be devastated, depleted, and depressed when you run out of self-confidence.

Decide right now that you'll put your confidence in Christ alone. That's the confidence that gets rewarded. That's the power that never runs out.

Jesus, I'm coming to You alone for strength and power. I realize my own strength won't get me very far. I put all my hope and confidence in You. I trust that You'll supply what I need when the time is right.

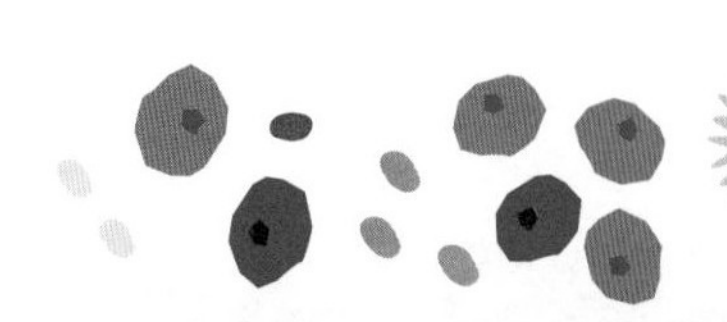

READY FOR ANYTHING

I can do everything through Christ, who gives me strength.
PHILIPPIANS 4:13 NLT

Have you heard today's verse before? It's a good one to know and memorize!

Take a look at how the Amplified Bible explains it: "I can do all things [which He has called me to do] through Him who strengthens and empowers me [to fulfill His purpose—I am self-sufficient in Christ's sufficiency; I am ready for anything and equal to anything through Him who infuses me with inner strength and confident peace.]" Isn't that a cool explanation? Maybe a little bit different than what you thought it meant?

You can do anything that *God has called you to do*, through *His* power. He is the one who gives you inner strength and confident peace. Take a minute and let that sink in. Because of Christ's Spirit at work in you, you can be completely confident that He is with you, making you ready for whatever comes your way. You don't have to be afraid. You don't have to worry. You don't have to dig down deep and try to find your own strength! You have His!

Lord, I'm thankful for Your strength at work inside me. Thanks for preparing me for everything that is coming my way.

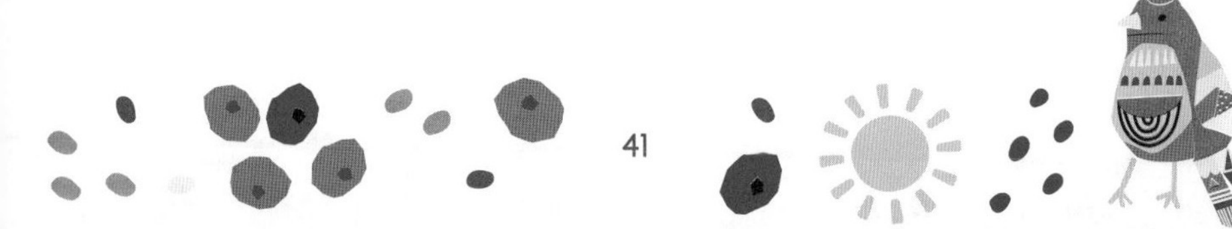

BIG PEOPLE OR BIG GOD?

So we can say with confidence, "The LORD is my helper, so I will have no fear. What can mere people do to me?"
HEBREWS 13:6 NLT

This mixed-up world makes it pretty easy to elevate people and forget about God. Social media and the news tell of people's greatness, but what about God? As Christians, we know that God is the Creator and the sustainer of all things. Check out Psalm 89:5–7 (NIV): "The heavens praise your wonders, LORD, your faithfulness too, in the assembly of the holy ones. For who in the skies above can compare with the LORD? Who is like the LORD among the heavenly beings? In the council of the holy ones God is greatly feared; he is more awesome than all who surround him."

God set all the stars in place and created the amazing human body. And He loves and cares for you personally! How amazing is that?

If you find yourself in a place where people have become big and difficult, humble yourself before God and set your heart and mind back on Him again. Look at His creation and praise Him for who He is. You can confidently say that God is bigger than anyone or anything you'll ever face.

Lord, I confess that people have become too big in my life. I repent of that and put You at the center of my life where You belong.

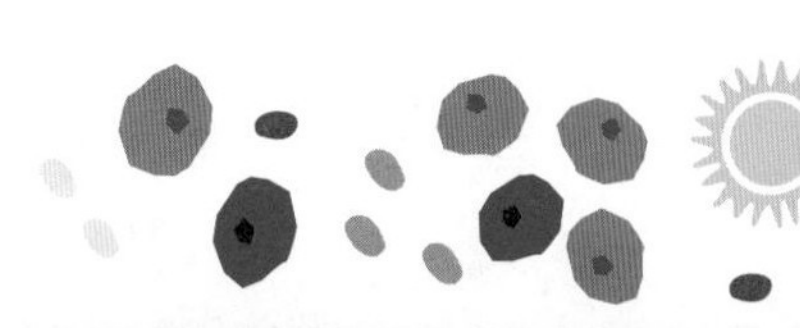

PSALM 23

Surely your goodness and unfailing love will pursue me all the days of my life, and I will live in the house of the LORD forever.

PSALM 23:6 NLT

Take out your Bible and turn to Psalm 23. The whole psalm is not very long and might take you only a minute or two to read. If you have a Bible app or another translation of the Bible around, try reading Psalm 23 in a few other translations. Reading the Bible in other translations can help you get a deeper meaning of the text.

The Twenty-Third Psalm is famous. People read it at funerals because it alludes to death and heaven. But it also has so much to do with life here and now. Read it slowly. Let it sink in and give you confidence that God is with you always. He restores and refreshes your soul. He is with you in the good and the bad. God's goodness, mercy, and love are available to you in every moment, and when you accept Him as Lord and leader of your life, you are guaranteed an eternity with Him in heaven.

Lord, You are my Good Shepherd. I follow along confidently because of Your goodness and great loving care for me. I trust that where we are going together is good and that You're with me no matter what happens along the way.

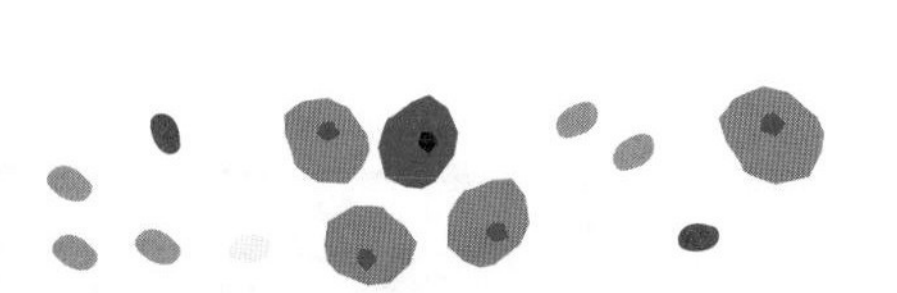

YOU'RE NOT A DIY PROJECT

In all my prayers for all of you, I always pray with joy because of your partnership in the gospel from the first day until now, being confident of this, that he who began a good work in you will carry it on to completion until the day of Christ Jesus.

PHILIPPIANS 1:4–6 NIV

Have you ever planned a fun project, got started, and then realized it was going to be a lot more work than you were hoping for? Did you finish? Or is that project in a pile with lots of other projects? Those DIY piles can get overwhelming!

Want to know something awesome? Jesus always finishes the projects He starts. He began a good work in you, and He plans to finish that! You are not a DIY project that Jesus started and then moved to the storage closet. You don't have to "do it yourself" if you want to grow more and more like Jesus. He set His Spirit in your heart to teach you, lead you, comfort you, and do the good work that Jesus started in you.

Need some extra confidence today? You can be confident of this: Jesus will finish the good work He started in you!

Thank You for placing Your Spirit in my heart, Lord Jesus! I'm thankful for the good work You're doing in me!

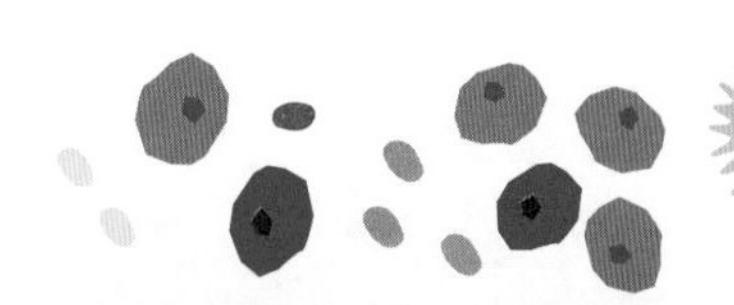

GOD'S PLANS

The Lord will work out his plans for my life—
for your faithful love, O Lord, endures forever.
Psalm 138:8 NLT

Dr. Ida Scudder was born in India a very long time ago. But her story is still important to young people today. Her parents were American missionaries who went to India to serve the people medically and spiritually. As a teen girl, Ida left and went to a private boarding school in the United States. She planned to get married and stay there when she graduated. She did not want to go back to India nor be a missionary!

But something happened that completely changed her mind. She was needed at home in India to help her dad with his medical practice when her mother got sick. When several women and babies died because their beliefs prevented male doctors from helping women, Ida knew then that God was calling her to help Indian women. She went on to become a doctor and opened her own hospital and medical school for women in India.

Just like Dr. Scudder, you can have confidence that God will work out His plans for your life for your good and His glory, even if you can't see or understand His plan just yet.

Lord, I'm thankful I don't have to be worried about my future. I know You have awesome plans for my life.

CONFIDENCE IN GOD'S LOVE

As we live in God, our love grows more perfect. So we will not be afraid on the day of judgment, but we can face him with confidence because we live like Jesus here in this world. Such love has no fear, because perfect love expels all fear. If we are afraid, it is for fear of punishment, and this shows that we have not fully experienced his perfect love.

1 John 4:17–18 NLT

Ask just about any mom, and she will tell you that no matter what kind of day she had with her child (good, bad, terrible), once that child goes to sleep at night, she will look upon them with love again. Good moms love their kids no matter what. And even if things were said and done during the day that caused anger and heartache, a loving mom forgives.

Moms are human, though, and don't always get everything right. How much more our perfect heavenly Father loves us. He never fails and always gets everything right. And His love is perfect.

If you have loving parents, thank God for them! And you can be confident that God loves you more than you could ever imagine. He loves you perfectly.

Lord, thanks for giving me a loving family.
Your perfect love is amazing to me.

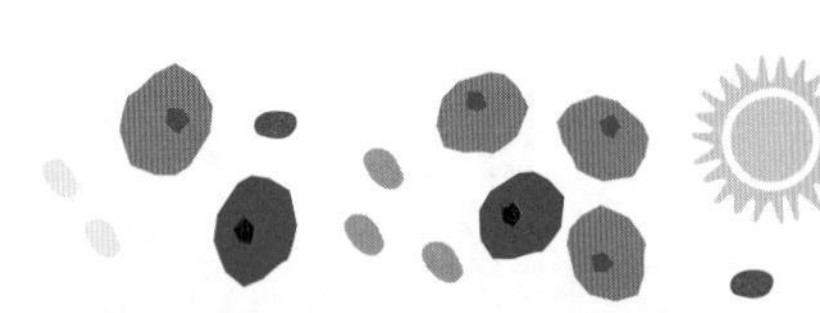

THE THRONE OF GRACE

Let us then approach God's throne of grace with confidence, so that we may receive mercy and find grace to help us in our time of need.

HEBREWS 4:16 NIV

You've probably seen a movie in which the common people bow before the king or queen. They have to get special permission to enter the palace and must have a very compelling reason to gain an audience with the ruler. The commoner is usually nervous and fearful as they present their requests to the king.

Because of Jesus and everything He did, you have full access to the King of kings. *The Message* says, "So let's walk right up to him and get what he is so ready to give. Take the mercy, accept the help."

You are God's beloved daughter, welcomed into the palace. You are royalty yourself. A seat is reserved for you in the grand banquet hall. So you can lift your head instead of cowering in fear. Jesus has made everything right for you before God. Approach His throne with confidence, knowing that you are covered in the righteousness of Christ.

Jesus, thank You for all You've done to make me right with God. It's because of You alone that I'm counted as royalty in God's kingdom.

NO WORRIES

"Do not worry about tomorrow, for tomorrow will worry about itself. Each day has enough trouble of its own."
MATTHEW 6:34 NIV

Have you ever spent a long time worrying about something that never actually happened? Think back to the last time you were really worried about something. Was it as bad as you thought it would be? It's amazing how creative our imaginations can be. We can imagine things way worse than they really are.

Katie was afraid of needles. But she knew she needed to get her blood sugar tested at her next medical exam because she was having some health problems. She made herself sick with worry about it and let it completely ruin her day. Guess what? When she got to the doctor's office, the nurse pricked her finger so fast that Katie hardly even knew it happened! She felt pretty silly getting all worried about something that was no big deal.

God doesn't want you to waste your life worrying about things that may or may not happen. He wants you to trust that He'll be with you no matter what.

Lord, I confess that I get worried about things that I don't understand and things that scare me. Help me learn to trust You more. I believe You're with me in all things.

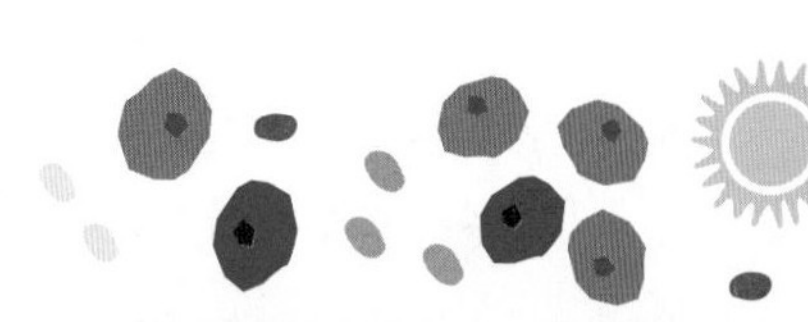

CONFIDENCE IN SCARY TIMES

"Do not fear, for I am with you; do not be dismayed,
for I am your God. I will strengthen you and help you;
I will uphold you with my righteous right hand."
ISAIAH 41:10 NIV

My daughter Jessa broke two bones in her leg last year and had to have surgery. Because of COVID-19, parents were only allowed to go into the prep room and couldn't go back to the surgery room at all. Jessa was wheeled through a set of large double doors, out of my sight, and we were both scared. If a person hasn't had anesthesia before, you never really know how they'll respond. She had never had any kind of surgery before and had never left me to go with strangers before either.

Her father and I prayed for Jessa before she went back into surgery, and I prayed the entire time in the waiting room. God was with us. We could sense it. He even sent a special hospital worker to meet us at the door that morning. She prayed with us and took us where we needed to go. The surgery went quickly, and before we knew it, the surgeon came out and said he was finished and that Jessa was recovering.

Lord, You are so good to comfort us when we're
afraid. Thanks for never leaving our side.

STRENGTH IN WEAKNESS

He said to me, "My grace is sufficient for you, for my power is made perfect in weakness." Therefore I will boast all the more gladly about my weaknesses, so that Christ's power may rest on me.
2 CORINTHIANS 12:9 NIV

Jessa had a long road of recovery after her surgery. She needed a wheelchair for a few months. She wasn't healing as well as the surgeon would have liked, and she spent a couple of months in physical therapy. She had to learn how to walk normally again. She had to work even harder at jumping and running—things that used to come naturally. Sadly, gymnastics was a thing of the past.

Jessa learned a lot about weakness and strength during those hard months. She had to give up a favorite sport. She had to learn to depend on God to strengthen her and heal her leg. Thankfully, after nearly a year, she made a full recovery, and a brand-new sport was waiting around the corner: volleyball! She quickly fell in love with it.

God uses hard things to teach us about His grace and power. When we're weak, He is strong!

Lord, thank You for healing us and giving us Your strength when we're weak.

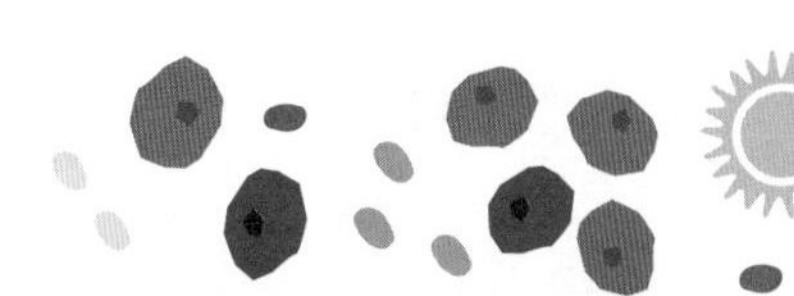

FIRM CONFIDENCE

The Lord will be your confidence, firm and strong, and will keep your foot from being caught [in a trap].
Proverbs 3:26 AMP

Does this verse mean your foot will literally never be caught or hurt? Nope. Jessa caught her foot on the wooden steps at a park and she fell. That's how she broke her leg.

Fear itself is the trap. Jessa could have been afraid of ever running and playing at that park again. Or she could have feared running itself! But she remembers that God brought good things out of her broken leg: people from all over prayed for her and supported her; she saw God's hand as He led the right people to meet us at the hospital and take care of her; and she was able to bless the new people she worked with at physical therapy and share God's love with them. She came out the other side stronger with a deeper trust in God and His healing.

You can be confident that God sees you. You don't have to be afraid of what's ahead, because you can trust that God will work everything out for your good and for His glory (see Romans 8:28).

My confidence is in You alone, Lord. I trust You are with me and working all things out for my good.

THE CONFIDENCE OF INTEGRITY

A wicked man puts on a bold face, but as for the upright, he considers, directs, and establishes his way [with the confidence of integrity].

Proverbs 21:29 AMP

It's been said that you should always tell the truth because the truth is easier to remember. That seems like common sense, right? Unless you're in the habit of lying. When you tell a lie, you often have to come up with a backstory and a cover-up. Lying becomes a tricky web that often gets the liar caught.

People of integrity are honest and trustworthy. They can be confident because they live in truth. They're not pretending or spinning webs of lies that are hard to remember.

Think of it this way: an honest person doesn't freak out when they're driving down the road and a police car pulls up behind them. They have nothing to fear because they know they haven't done anything wrong. But someone who is in the habit of lying and trying to get away with things will often get that feeling in the pit of their stomach that they're about to be found out when a person of authority comes around.

Lord Jesus, I want to be a girl of integrity. Give me courage and wisdom to be an honest and truthful person.

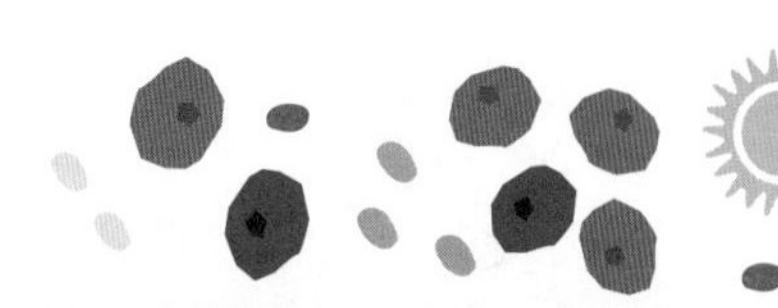

TRUE VALUE

Because of the privilege and authority God has given me, I give each of you this warning: Don't think you are better than you really are. Be honest in your evaluation of yourselves, measuring yourselves by the faith God has given us.

ROMANS 12:3 NLT

Have you ever met someone who brags about her abilities? Maybe she is super talented, but it's not fun to be around her, right? Be gracious with her. Remember this: that person most likely hasn't been taught how valuable and loved by God she really is. Our value has nothing to do with our talent and abilities.

The Message says it this way: "Living then, as every one of you does, in pure grace, it's important that you not misinterpret yourselves as people who are bringing this goodness to God. No, God brings it all to you. The only accurate way to understand ourselves is by what God is and by what he does for us, not by what we are and what we do for him."

When you come across someone who brags about her abilities, pray for her to come to know that her true value comes from God, who loves and cherishes her even if all her talent is stripped away.

Lord, help me see people like You do and to share Your love with them.

WHAT OTHERS THINK

The fear of human opinion disables;
trusting in God protects you from that.
Proverbs 29:25 MSG

There are many people in this world (not just kids and teens, but full-grown adults!) who are totally obsessed with what other people think about them. Just spend two minutes on social media, and you'll see this to be true. Many people worry so much about what others think that it paralyzes them with fear. They're afraid to use their gifts and talents because they're worried about what other people might say about them.

The alternative to this is the fear of God. This doesn't mean a "cower in fear because God is going to punish you" kind of fear. This is a "trust in God because He's all-powerful and awesome" kind of fear of the Lord. Make sense?

God made you just the way you are with special talents and abilities to brighten up a dark world. God created you the way you are on purpose. So take a loooong break from your phone and start doing the things God created you to do. Go out and make Him smile, no matter what anyone else says.

Lord God, I confess I worry about what others
think too much. Please help me to be confident in
You and to be the girl You created me to be!

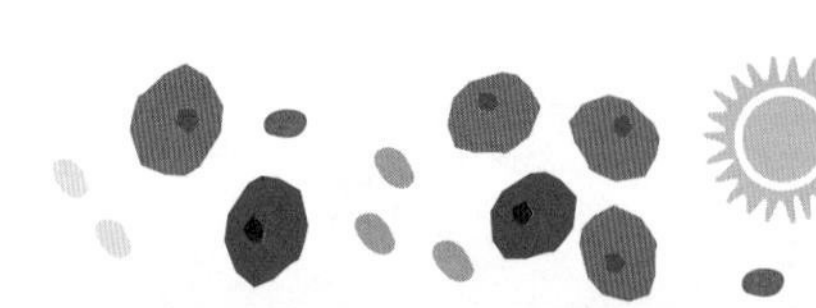

THE FEAR OF GOD

The Fear-of-God builds up confidence,
and makes a world safe for your children.
PROVERBS 14:26 MSG

The Amplified Bible says it this way: "In the [reverent] fear of the LORD there is strong confidence, and His children will [always] have a place of refuge." The Bible also tells us that the fear of God is the beginning of wisdom (Proverbs 9:10). That doesn't mean we are afraid to approach God. No! We are able to boldly go into God's presence because of Jesus (Ephesians 3:12; Hebrews 4:16). But fearing God means that we honor our holy, awesome, and all-powerful God, and we have no other idols before Him. We don't put other people in God's place. Is there anything or any person you need to lay down before God so that He can take His rightful spot in your life?

Remember that God is our safe hiding place—our refuge. When you are afraid of anything, you can always run to Him for help and safety. What are you feeling scared of today? Bring it to Jesus in prayer.

Lord God, You are awesome and all-powerful. I come before You in reverence yet boldly because of Jesus. Please highlight and remove any idols in my life that are hindering my relationship with You.

THE FEAR OF MAN

I came to you in weakness with great fear and trembling. My message and my preaching were not with wise and persuasive words, but with a demonstration of the Spirit's power, so that your faith might not rest on human wisdom, but on God's power.

1 Corinthians 2:3–5 NIV

Certain people can seem downright scary sometimes. An angry kid at school. A teacher you have trouble with. A bully. Even though being around that person might feel intimidating, remember that God is bigger!

Let's take a look at Hebrews 13:6 (NLT) again! "We can say with confidence, 'The Lord is my helper, so I will have no fear. What can mere people do to me?'"

Write this verse down and post it where you can see it every day. Trust that God has power over everything and every person. When you bring that intimidating person before God, He can help!

Take a moment now and bring to mind any person in your life that makes you a little bit scared. Ask Him to give you His perspective of that person. Put God back on the throne of your heart and mind, where He belongs. He will give you confidence to deal with all the people in your life.

Lord, I don't want to give any person power over my life. You are the King of my heart and mind.

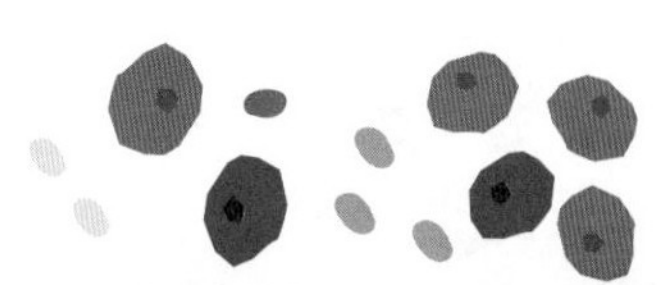

COURAGE AND CONFIDENCE

While they were praying, the place where they were meeting trembled and shook. They were all filled with the Holy Spirit and continued to speak God's Word with fearless confidence.
ACTS 4:31 MSG

The "early church" consisted of Jesus' followers in the time period right after Jesus' death and resurrection. The early church was being persecuted by the Jewish council, and Jesus' disciples Peter and John were put in prison for telling others about Jesus. But because they were filled with the Holy Spirit, they kept on telling others about the love and power of God through Jesus Christ. Acts 4:13 (NIV) says, "When [the Jewish rulers] saw the courage of Peter and John and realized that they were unschooled, ordinary men, they were astonished and they took note that these men had been with Jesus."

When God speaks to you and calls you to do something scary, you can know for sure that He will equip you and give you the strength and courage to do what He's asking you to. Even if you feel ordinary and unexceptional, being with Jesus will give you all the courage you need.

Lord Jesus, I want others to be able to tell that I've been spending time with You. Thanks for giving me all the courage and confidence I need.

AM I RIGHT?

Let the one who thinks he stands firm [immune to temptation, being overconfident and self-righteous], take care that he does not fall [into sin and condemnation].
1 Corinthians 10:12 AMP

Today's scripture is a good reminder to put your confidence in Jesus instead of in yourself. *The Message* says it this way: "Forget about self-confidence; it's useless. Cultivate God-confidence."

It's really easy to give in to pride when you think you're doing a good job or if you think you're 100 percent right about something—am I right? I know a young couple who got into a silly fight over a character in a movie when they were first married. The wife was 100 percent sure that she knew the actor's name. The husband was 100 percent sure that she was wrong. But he was a bit humbler about it. This turned into an argument that went on for hours until they finally researched the correct answer. The wife was wrong, and she felt very ashamed because her pride caused her to scoff at and belittle her husband. She had some apologizing to do.

The lesson here? Even if you're pretty sure you're right, be humble and kind. Don't let pride interfere with your relationships.

Lord, I want to be humble and kind instead of full of pride. Please help me.

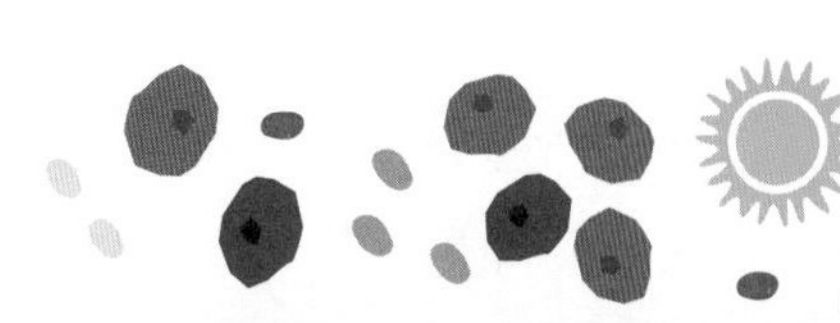

TALKING TO JESUS

May the Master pour on the love so it fills your lives and splashes over on everyone around you, just as it does from us to you. May you be infused with strength and purity, filled with confidence in the presence of God our Father when our Master Jesus arrives with all his followers.

1 Thessalonians 3:12–13 MSG

Jesus was traveling and went through Samaria. Most Jews avoided traveling through this town, and they avoided Samaritan people too. Samaritans and Jews did not get along. In fact, the Jews hated the mixed-race people of Samaria. But a Samaritan woman was drawing water from the well when Jesus was there. Jesus knew everything about her, of course. She was likely ashamed of her life and all the bad choices she made. Scholars say that that's why she was getting water in the middle of the day rather than in the cool of the morning—to avoid other women who would judge and condemn her.

Jesus didn't condemn her. He spoke truth and love to her, offering her living water. This woman who came to the well alone suddenly had the courage to run into town and tell everyone about Jesus (John 4:28–29). Talking to Jesus can give you confidence like that too.

Thank You for Your great love for me, Lord.
Allow it to splash over on those around me.

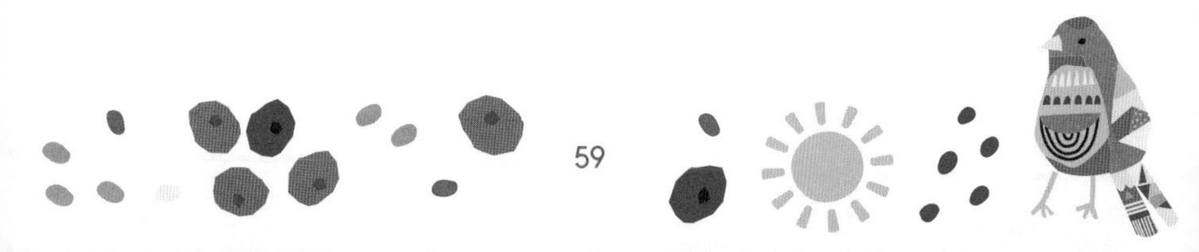

EYES TO SEE

He touched their eyes, saying, "According to your faith [your trust and confidence in My power and My ability to heal] it will be done to you."
MATTHEW 9:29 AMP

Two blind men were following Jesus in the streets. They were calling out to Him, "Have mercy on us, Son of David!" (Matthew 9:27 NIV). Jesus didn't turn around and heal them immediately. But the blind men followed and got close to Jesus. Then Jesus asked them if they believed He really could heal them. When they said they did believe, Jesus touched their eyes and they could see!

Jesus could have healed everyone who was alive in the world as He walked the streets in Bible times, but He didn't. He waited for people to come to Him and believe. That's still true today. Do you have trust and confidence in the power of Jesus? Is there anything blocking your ability to trust in what God can do? Talk to Jesus about this today. Ask Him to touch the eyes of your heart so that you can see all He is doing in your life.

Lord Jesus, I believe in You. Help me trust confidently in Your power and ability to heal. Please open my eyes to see all the ways You are at work in my life.

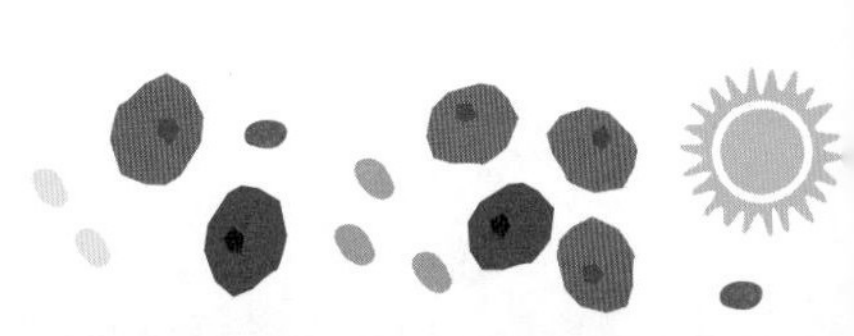

DAVID AND GOLIATH

The Lord is my strength and my [impenetrable] shield;
my heart trusts [with unwavering confidence] in Him,
and I am helped; therefore my heart greatly rejoices,
and with my song I shall thank Him and praise Him.
Psalm 28:7 AMP

Before King David was a king, he was only a shepherd boy, the youngest of all his brothers. Some of David's brothers were warriors, trained in battle with armor and swords. David defended his sheep with a slingshot and a staff.

When a champion named Goliath came and threatened the Israelites, everyone was terrified to go up against the giant. Everyone but David, that is. David volunteered to go and fight Goliath, knowing that God would be with him. He faced the giant warrior with five stones, his slingshot, and his confidence in almighty God.

When the Philistine taunted David, he replied, "You come to me with sword, spear, and javelin, but I come to you in the name of the Lord of Heaven's Armies—the God of the armies of Israel, whom you have defied" (1 Samuel 17:45 NLT).

Do you know how the story ends? Yep! God won! The same God who was with David is with you in every moment too.

Lord, I'm thankful for the Bible and the true stories that show me how great and powerful You are! Thanks for giving me confidence.

GIDEON'S STORY

O my God, in You I [have unwavering] trust [and I rely on You with steadfast confidence], do not let me be ashamed or my hope in You be disappointed; do not let my enemies triumph over me.

PSALM 25:2 AMP

Gideon's story is found in the Old Testament book of Judges. He was afraid of the Midianites, a neighboring people who oppressed the Israelites. But God chose Gideon to rescue Israel from the tyranny of the Midianites. He sent the Angel of the Lord to tell Gideon what to do.

In Judges 6:15–16 (NLT), Gideon said to God, "How can I rescue Israel? My clan is the weakest in the whole tribe of Manasseh, and I am the least in my entire family!"

But God promised Gideon that He would be with him. Then, through a miraculous series of events, God caused Gideon's tiny army of three hundred men to defeat thousands of Midianites. The Midianites were so panicky at the end that they even started fighting one another.

God used Gideon to show that He can use anyone who puts their trust in Him. When you rely on God for your confidence, you will always be in the very best hands.

My life is in Your hands, Lord. I put all my trust and confidence in You.

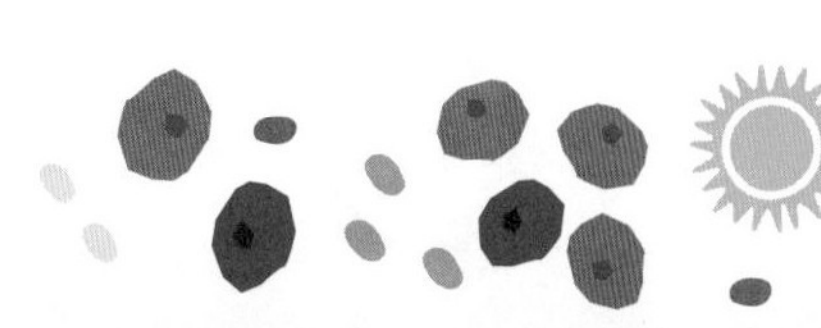

EVERY STEP

For You are my hope; O Lord God, You are my trust and the source of my confidence from my youth.

Psalm 71:5 AMP

Jeremiah was an Old Testament prophet. The Bible says that God set him apart before he was even born and appointed him as a prophet (Jeremiah 1:4–5). Jeremiah responded by saying, "I do not know how to speak; I am only a child." And here's what God said: "Don't say, 'I'm too young,' for you must go wherever I send you and say whatever I tell you. And don't be afraid of the people, for I will be with you and will protect you. I, the Lord, have spoken!" (Jeremiah 1:7–8 NLT).

Just as God knew Jeremiah before he was born, God also knew you. He set you apart for a reason, chosen to be His beloved child. Isn't that awesome? When you feel down and discouraged and can't wait to grow up or move on with your life, remember this: God has you right where you are for a purpose. Listen as He leads you. He promises to be with you every step of the way!

I'm thankful to know that You've chosen me as Your child, Lord God. Fill me with Your life and love as I go through each stage of life with You by my side and in my heart.

THE NAME ABOVE ALL NAMES

I will say of the Lord, "He is my refuge and my fortress, my God, in whom I trust [with great confidence, and on whom I rely]!"
Psalm 91:2 AMP

Did you know that the name of Jesus is powerful? Philippians 2:9–11 (NLT) says, "Therefore, God elevated him to the place of highest honor and gave him the name above all other names, that at the name of Jesus every knee should bow, in heaven and on earth and under the earth, and every tongue declare that Jesus Christ is Lord, to the glory of God the Father."

Sometimes the most effective prayer in a difficult moment is simply: "Jesus!"

A group of college girls was traveling on a mission trip, and as they were driving on the highway around a mountain, the driver was momentarily distracted and drove into the other lane as a semitruck came barreling along. The director of the group watched this happen, being in the car right behind them. In fear, he simply cried out, "Jesus!" Thankfully, no one was hurt in that scary incident.

When you call on the name of Jesus for help, you are trusting in His power over all things. Say His name. He is your mighty fortress.

Jesus, Lord of all, I'm thankful I can call on You at all times for help!

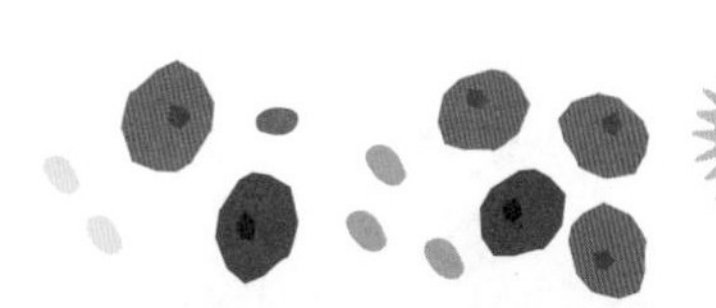

GOD SUPPLIES THE HELP

Then the LORD asked Moses, "Who makes a person's mouth? Who decides whether people speak or do not speak, hear or do not hear, see or do not see? Is it not I, the LORD? Now go! I will be with you as you speak, and I will instruct you in what to say."
EXODUS 4:11–12 NLT

God called Moses to lead His people out of Egypt. Moses did not want this assignment. I repeat: Moses did not want this assignment! Here's what he said to God: "Lord, please! Send anyone else" (Exodus 4:13 NLT).

Moses complained to God, telling Him that he wasn't a good speaker and was easily tongue-tied. He pleaded with God not to make him do this. But God promised to be with him and give him the right words to say. He even let Moses take his brother, Aaron, along with him to be his mouthpiece.

If you're facing something difficult, remember that God is with you. He will send you all the help you need. Jesus is at work in you, carrying your heavy burdens and supplying the strength you need for whatever task God has called you to do.

Lord God, I bring You all the hard things I'm facing. I trust You are at work in me, giving me strength and confidence to do what You ask.

WALKING IN CONFIDENCE

The Lord God is my strength [my source of courage, my invincible army]; He has made my feet [steady and sure] like hinds' feet and makes me walk [forward with spiritual confidence] on my high places [of challenge and responsibility].

Habakkuk 3:19 AMP

The story of Queen Esther in the Old Testament is one of courage and God-confidence. Esther, a Jew, became queen of Persia. Even though she was queen, she had very few rights and little power as a woman. But Esther found favor with the king. When she learned that her people were in grave danger of being annihilated, she risked her life to help save them. She walked forward with confidence and made her requests known to the king. The king granted her request. God had set her in a position to help at just the right time.

If God is asking you to do something that seems hard—maybe to lead a Bible study at school or share the love of Jesus with a friend who doesn't know Him—you can trust that He will give you courage and help you walk forward in confidence.

Lord, help me walk forward in confidence when You call me to do things that seem hard. I know You're with me. Help me trust You more.

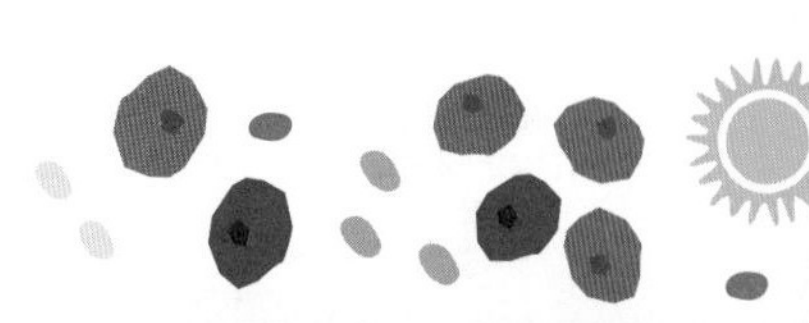

IN DESPERATION

So, friends, take a firm stand, feet on the ground and head high. Keep a tight grip on what you were taught, whether in personal conversation or by our letter. May Jesus himself and God our Father, who reached out in love and surprised you with gifts of unending help and confidence, put a fresh heart in you, invigorate your work, enliven your speech.

2 Thessalonians 2:15–17 MSG

A desperate woman came up to Jesus from behind, believing that if she could just touch His cloak, she would be healed. Because of her bleeding problem, she was considered "unclean" and "untouchable." She was an outcast. She reached out her hand to touch Jesus' cloak and probably thought she could slip quietly away. Mark 5:29 (NIV) says, "Immediately her bleeding stopped and she felt in her body that she was freed from her suffering."

But Jesus called out to her. He told her that her faith in Him had healed her.

This desperate woman had the confidence to go into a crowd and reach out for Jesus. Desperation can make you do some unusual things. Have you ever felt desperate enough to do something you normally wouldn't do? Take those desperate feelings to Jesus and watch as He reaches out in love to you with "unending help and confidence."

Lord, You are so good and loving. Thank You for helping me and giving me confidence.

THE CONFIDENCE TO ASK

If you need wisdom, ask our generous God, and he will give it to you. He will not rebuke you for asking.

James 1:5 NLT

Girl, you're gonna need a whole lot of wisdom to survive and thrive in this crazy world! The great news is that Jesus wants to give it to you. You simply have to ask! James 1:5 says to ask our generous God for wisdom and He'll give it to you! It's that simple.

Think of any situation you have right now that feels overwhelming. You're not sure what to do. There are so many choices you could make. Is something causing you stress or anxiety? Bring it to your mind and talk to Jesus about it. Ask Him for wisdom. Picture Jesus standing in front of you and talk to Him about your situation. He is generous and wants to help. Close your eyes and imagine Him with you. What does He want you to know? Ask Jesus to exchange your fears and anxieties for His wisdom, power, and peace.

Jesus, I'm thankful that You want to give me wisdom! Please replace my fears and anxieties with Your power and purpose. Please fill me with peace in Your presence. I want to hear from You. I want to live a life set apart for You.

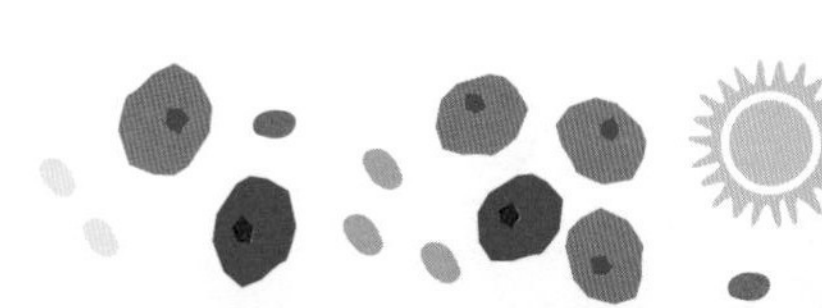

FEARLESS CONFIDENCE

So that your trust and reliance and confidence may be in the Lord, I have taught these things to you today, even to you.
Proverbs 22:19 AMP

Imagine firemen rushing into a burning building with fearless confidence. Adrenaline is pulsing through their bodies, helping them act courageously and quickly to get the job done, save any victims, and put out the fire.

If God gives you a mission like that, you can be confident that He'll equip you. God created our amazing bodies to pump with adrenaline and accomplish things a human couldn't normally do when we're in tense and dangerous situations like emergency personnel face. Our bodies are designed to release adrenaline to initiate our fight-or-flight response when we face high stress. Isn't that cool?

But even if you never run into a burning building, you can trust that God will help you do what He has called you to do. The Creator of our amazing human bodies is the God who sees you. He knows your name. He made you on purpose. He calls and equips every one of His children for His plan and purpose.

Lord, I trust that fearless confidence comes from You alone. I know You're with me always and I can rely on You for wisdom, courage, and strength. Thanks for equipping me to do anything You call me to do.

JOY

"I saw the Lord always before me. Because he is at my right hand, I will not be shaken. Therefore my heart is glad and my tongue rejoices; my body also will rest in hope, because you will not abandon me to the realm of the dead, you will not let your holy one see decay. You have made known to me the paths of life; you will fill me with joy in your presence."

ACTS 2:25–28 NIV

You've probably heard that old children's church song that goes like this: "I've got the joy, joy, joy, joy down in my heart. Where? Down in my heart. . ."

Is that song going through your head right now? And maybe for the rest of the day? You're welcome! It's a good one to get stuck in your head.

Why? Because joy is important. You need to know what it is, where it comes from, and what joy's purpose is. It'll help you get through your great life adventure.

We're going to be talking a lot about joy in the coming days. Get ready to sing and worship, for joy comes in the morning (Psalm 30:5)!

Father, Your Word promises that You'll fill me with joy in Your presence. I'm excited about that—and thankful! I'm looking forward to knowing more about the joy that You bring to my life.

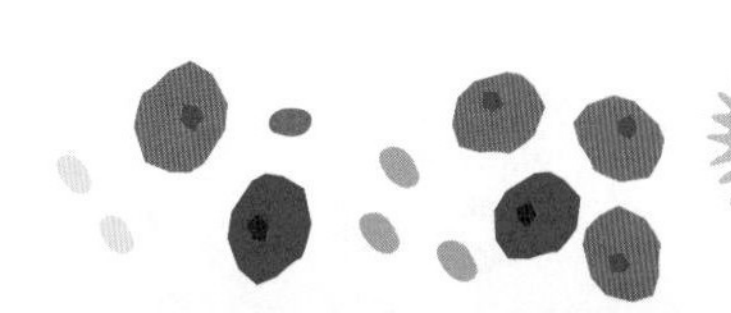

JOY TO THE WORLD

"Until now you have not asked [the Father] for anything in My name; but now ask and keep on asking and you will receive, so that your joy may be full and complete."
JOHN 16:24 AMP

Joy to the world, the Lord is come.
Let earth receive her King.
Let every heart prepare Him room
And heaven and nature sing.

There you have it—another song stuck in your head for the day!

"Joy to the World" is one of the most famous Christmas carols we sing every December in anticipation of the day we celebrate Christ's birth. Interestingly enough, the author of the song intended for the lyrics to depict Christ's second coming rather than the first. A little bit of research shows that the song was based partially on Psalm 98 in which we see a call to shout and sing together for joy.

Regardless of what the author originally intended, it's a great song to sing any time of year. It reminds us where our joy comes from—our King, Jesus!

Are you preparing room in your heart for Him?

Jesus, please clear out anything in my heart that is getting in the way of our relationship. I want to be filled with Your supernatural joy.

HAPPINESS AND JOY

I have told you these things, so that in Me you may have [perfect] peace. In the world you have tribulation and distress and suffering, but be courageous [be confident, be undaunted, be filled with joy]; I have overcome the world." [My conquest is accomplished, My victory abiding.]

John 16:33 AMP

Joy often gets confused with the emotion of happiness. People are happy when good things are happening. But joy is different. Joy is a gift from God that has nothing to do with our circumstances.

First Chronicles 16:27 (AMP) says, "Splendor and majesty are [found] in His presence; strength and joy are [found] in His place (sanctuary)."

If you're looking for joy, the place you need to go and find it is in God's sanctuary, the place where He dwells. And where does God dwell? Not in temples built by human hands, but in your heart. That's the place where you meet with God. If you've chosen to follow Him, His dwelling place is your heart.

As you spend time in God's presence, praying, reading His Word, worshipping Him in good times and bad, He fills you with joy, no matter what you may be going through.

Lord, I'm thankful that no matter what I'm going through, You offer me joy and peace in Your powerful presence. Thank You for meeting with me in Your dwelling place—my heart.

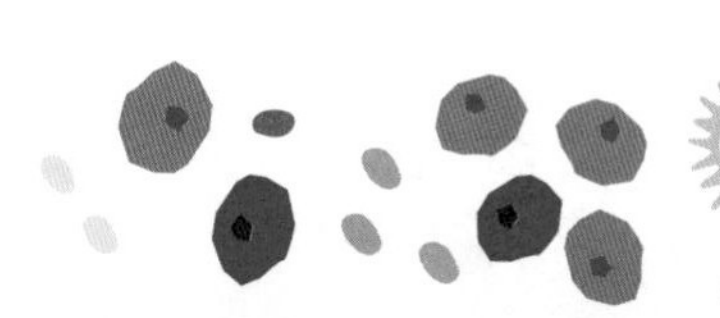

REJOICE IN THE LORD ALWAYS

Rejoice in the Lord always [delight, take pleasure in Him]; again I will say, rejoice!
PHILIPPIANS 4:4 AMP

Are you a content girl, or do you find yourself often wishing for the next thing? Ask God to give you contentment today, regardless of your circumstances. You can make it through anything with the Spirit of the living God at work inside you.

Take a look at Philippians 4:12–13 (MSG): "I've learned by now to be quite content whatever my circumstances. I'm just as happy with little as with much, with much as with little. I've found the recipe for being happy whether full or hungry, hands full or hands empty. Whatever I have, wherever I am, I can make it through anything in the One who makes me who I am."

If you're having trouble feeling God's supernatural peace and joy, the problem could be a lack of contentment. Ask God to fill you with contentment, thankfulness, and joy even if you're struggling with hard times. This doesn't mean you ignore your feelings or pretend that everything is okay when it isn't. Instead, bring all those thoughts and feelings to the only one who can help. Turn on the praise music and begin to worship the source of joy and peace.

I worship You, Lord, no matter what. Fill me with contentment and peace while I praise You!

GOODNESS, PEACE, AND JOY

For the Kingdom of God is not a matter of what we eat or drink, but of living a life of goodness and peace and joy in the Holy Spirit.
ROMANS 14:17 NLT

When we commit our lives to Jesus, the Holy Spirit comes to live inside our hearts and works in us to carry out God's plans here on earth. Ephesians 1:19–20 (NLT) says, "I [Paul] also pray that you will understand the incredible greatness of God's power for us who believe him. This is the same mighty power that raised Christ from the dead and seated him in the place of honor at God's right hand in the heavenly realms."

The Holy Spirit's mighty power is working inside of you today. Isn't that amazing?

Jesus promised us in John 14 that His Holy Spirit is here to comfort us, teach us, and remind us of everything that Jesus said. Seek Him and allow His love and supernatural power to lead and guide you with goodness, peace, and joy.

Jesus, I'm thankful for Your Spirit alive inside me. I can't comprehend the power that I have access to because of You and Your great love for me. I want a life of goodness, peace, and joy in Your presence. Thanks for making me Your child.

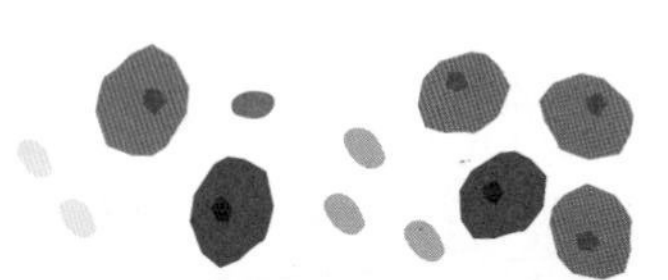

CARRY IT TO JESUS

Be joyful in hope, patient in affliction, faithful in prayer.
ROMANS 12:12 NIV

In Matthew 11:28–30 (NIV), Jesus said, "Come to me, all you who are weary and burdened, and I will give you rest. Take my yoke upon you and learn from me, for I am gentle and humble in heart, and you will find rest for your souls. For my yoke is easy and my burden is light."

When you carry your burdens to Jesus, He exchanges your heaviness for rest, peace, and joy in His presence. He gives you an eternal perspective where you can see problems and heartache in their proper light. Weeping may last for a little while, but joy will come (Psalm 30:5). The rest Jesus gives is supernatural, providing joy and strength to do the next thing.

Are you struggling right now, my friend? Bring any sadness or heartache to Jesus. Picture yourself carrying it all to Him. Take a few moments now in prayer and picture yourself carrying your heavy load to Jesus. He is with you.

Lord Jesus, I bring all of my worries and heartache to You now. I've carried it for too long without coming to You. Your Word says You'll give me rest. I lay all of this down and take You up on Your promise.

FRIENDS OF GOD

"These things I have spoken to you, that my joy may be in you, and that your joy may be full."
JOHN 15:11 ESV

In the Old Testament, a face-to-face relationship with God wasn't possible for most people. Jesus hadn't come for us yet. Moses was favored and chosen by God to lead, so God spent special, face-to-face time with Moses while the others looked on. God spoke to Moses just like a friend. Through bearing our sins on the cross, Jesus made a way for all of us to have a special, face-to-face relationship with God.

John 15:15 (NIV) says, "I no longer call you servants, because a servant does not know his master's business. Instead, I have called you friends, for everything that I learned from my Father I have made known to you."

A face-to-face friendship with God is not something to take for granted. Remember, it wasn't even possible for most people back in Moses' time. Now God has chosen you to be His friend. Allow that fact to fill you with joy!

Father, I'm honored and amazed that You call me Your friend, all because of Jesus taking my punishment on the cross. Thank You for making a way for us to be friends.

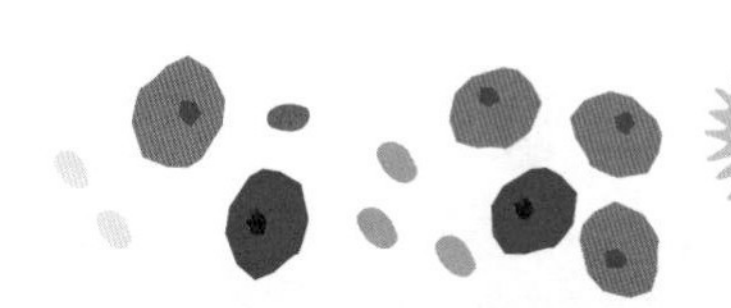

TIME TO WORSHIP

All you saints! Sing your hearts out to God! Thank him to his face!
He gets angry once in a while, but across a lifetime there is only love.
The nights of crying your eyes out give way to days of laughter.
Psalm 30:4–5 MSG

The New Living Translation says, "Weeping may last through the night, but joy comes with the morning." Quite a few songs have been based on this psalm. Joy comes in the morning. Even if life seems hard right now in the middle of difficult circumstances, a new season is coming. Joy is just around the corner as you spend time in God's presence.

So let's take time right now to worship God. Praise Him for who He is and what He has done. Colossians 1:15 tells us that Jesus is the image of the invisible God. Picture Jesus in your mind's eye. Belt out your favorite worship song and picture Jesus receiving your praise. Sing your heart out to God. He is worthy of all your worship and adoration. He is ready to bless you with joy as you spend time in His presence.

Lord, I worship You today because of who You are! You are good and loving. You're my Creator and the lover of my soul— the God of all. Every good thing I have is because of You.

LET US REJOICE

This is the day that the LORD has made; let us rejoice and be glad in it.
PSALM 118:24 ESV

Here's another Sunday school song to hum along with today:

This is the day, this is the day,
That the Lord has made, that the Lord has made.
I will rejoice, I will rejoice
And be glad in it, and be glad in it!

As you start your morning, thank God for the gift of life and the blessing of a new day. Whatever happened yesterday is in the past. Move forward in joy with Jesus by your side and in your heart.

First Chronicles 16:10–11 (AMP) says, "Let the hearts of those who seek the LORD rejoice. Seek the LORD and His strength; seek His face continually [longing to be in His presence]."

Is your heart seeking God today? Start your morning off right. Seek the Lord's face, worship Him, and ask Him to fill you with His strength for whatever you're facing today. You don't have to be afraid of what's ahead, because He'll never leave you. Rejoice in that truth!

Lord, thank You for the gift of this new day! Please give me a deep desire and a longing to know You more and to spend time with You in Your Word and in prayer.

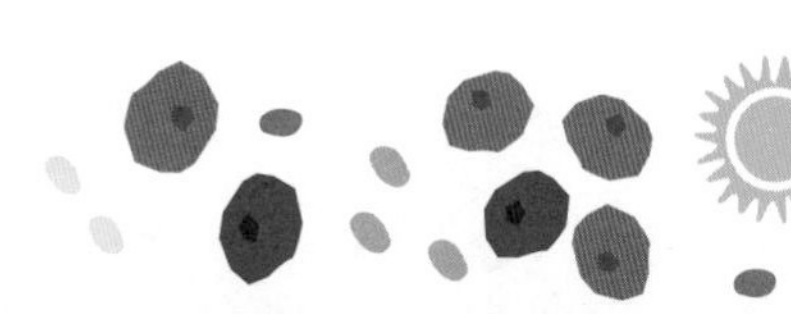

THE JOY OF THE LORD

"This day is holy to our Lord. Do not grieve,
for the joy of the LORD is your strength."
NEHEMIAH 8:10 NIV

The world God created was a beautiful place, but because of sin, it is now a messed-up place that has lost much of its splendor. We live in a fallen world, and things won't be perfect again until Jesus returns to set things right for eternity. In John 16:33 (NLT), Jesus said, "I have told you all this so that you may have peace in me. Here on earth you will have many trials and sorrows. But take heart, because I have overcome the world."

Jesus said that in this world we will have trouble because it's not heaven. We can't expect it to be. He promised in John 14:27 (NIV), "Peace I leave with you; my peace I give you. I do not give to you as the world gives. Do not let your hearts be troubled and do not be afraid."

These are verses to write down and ask the Holy Spirit to help you remember! The world says that peace must be the absence of problems. But that's not what Jesus said. He said that perfect peace is His presence and power in the midst of problems. The joy of the Lord is your strength!

Thank You for Your truth, Lord. Help me believe it and live my life by it!

OUR LIVING HOPE

The hope of the righteous [those of honorable character and integrity] is joy, but the expectation of the wicked [those who oppose God and ignore His wisdom] comes to nothing.

PROVERBS 10:28 AMP

When a believer in Christ dies, the following scripture is often used as a comfort: "We do not want you to be uninformed, believers, about those who are asleep [in death], so that you will not grieve [for them] as the others do who have no hope [beyond this present life]" (1 Thessalonians 4:13 AMP).

As Christians, we have God's eternal Word at our fingertips—access to the truth of what's to come. We have a living hope. But those who don't know Christ have no hope beyond this present life. If you spend five minutes reading the news, you'll see the panic and uncertainty of a world with no hope.

Jesus is our living hope, now and forever. As this truth fills you with joy throughout your lifetime, others will see it and want to know the hope and joy you have. Be ready to share the love and joy of Jesus with them!

Jesus, You're my living hope—alive in me now and for all eternity! I'm full of joy and hope because of You. Give me courage to share my faith with others who need Your hope.

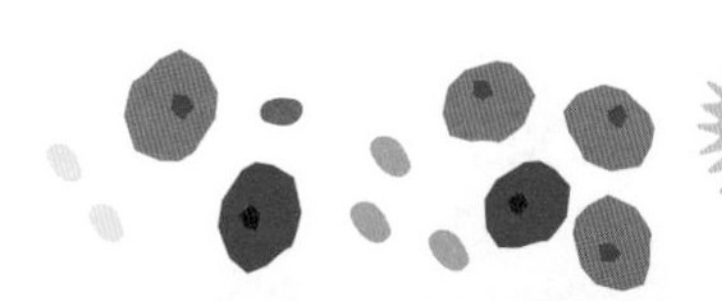

CREATED TO WORSHIP

Let all who take refuge and put their trust in You rejoice, let them ever sing for joy; because You cover and shelter them, let those who love Your name be joyful and exult in You.

Psalm 5:11 AMP

The biblical meaning of worship is to "bow down" and give honor to someone who is worthy. All people were created with the ability to worship. Humans who don't worship God usually worship their lesser idols: phones, clothes, people, entertainment, and so on.

As a child of God, you were created to worship Him. Revelation 5:13 (NLT) says, "Then I heard every creature in heaven and on earth and under the earth and in the sea. They sang: 'Blessing and honor and glory and power belong to the one sitting on the throne and to the Lamb forever and ever.'"

Worship is a powerful thing. It gets your mind off of yourself and your problems and sets it on God, the Author and Creator of life itself. Turn on your praise music today and worship Jesus in your heart and mind. Then watch the joy roll in!

I worship You alone, Lord. You are good and holy and all-powerful. Thank You for taking care of me. I put all my trust in You!

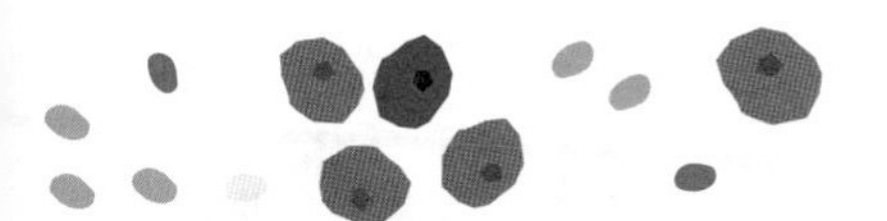

SPREADING JOY

When he arrived and saw this evidence of God's blessing, he was filled with joy, and he encouraged the believers to stay true to the Lord. Barnabas was a good man, full of the Holy Spirit and strong in faith. And many people were brought to the Lord.

ACTS 11:23–24 NLT

Barnabas was a nickname given to one of the early missionaries. The name *Barnabas* means "Son of Encouragement." Barnabas traveled with Paul, and his story is told in the book of Acts. Barnabas was known for being a great encourager. He was full of the Holy Spirit, and God used him greatly to change people's lives.

Can you think of someone in your life who is really good at encouraging others? How does that person make you feel? A good encourager builds up other people and points them to Jesus. Encouragers offer words of hope and life and joy.

Take some time to ask God who you might encourage today. Make a list of the people in your life and ask God to show you how to bless and encourage those people at just the right time.

Lord, I want to be an encourager! I want to spread Your hope and joy to the people who need it. Show me how I can do that, and please give me courage and resources to make it happen.

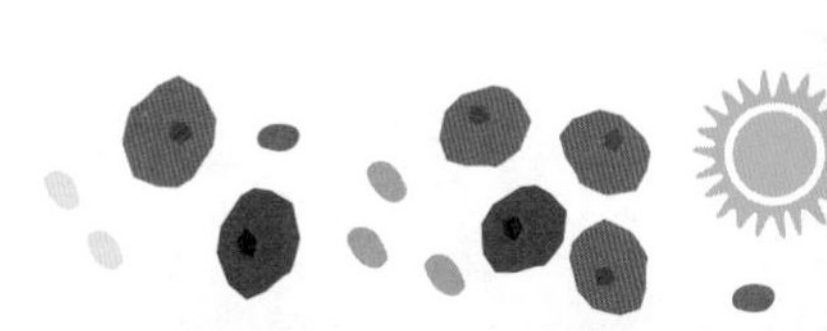

SOWING AND REAPING

Those who sow with tears will reap with songs of joy.
PSALM 126:5 NIV

Has anyone in your family planted a garden before? For the past two years, our family has experimented with a large garden plot. It has been fun to research all the plants and the best way to care for them. The first year, we didn't know what we were doing at all. We had no idea how quickly weeds could grow and overwhelm a garden (and a person! Whew!). There may or may not have been some tears involved.

This year, we followed a seasoned, large-garden YouTuber and took her advice about weeds. We bought a special weed-control fabric, and it worked wonders! We had a huge crop and minimal weeds.

Sowing and reaping is a biblical concept that you'll find throughout the pages of scripture. Galatians 6:7 (NIV) tells us, "A man reaps what he sows." Today's scripture in Psalm 126 is a beautiful reminder that God is close to the brokenhearted (see Psalm 34:18). And even if what you've planted is coming up different than what you expected or seems overwhelming, joy will come as you stay close to the Master Gardener: Jesus.

Lord, I'm thankful that You are with me in every season. Draw me closer to You, Jesus.

FRUIT TREES AND REAL LIFE

Those who go out weeping, carrying seed to sow, will return with songs of joy, carrying sheaves with them.
Psalm 126:6 NIV

This next verse in Psalm 126 continues with the gardening theme. *The Message* says it this way: "And now, God, do it again—bring rains to our drought-stricken lives so those who planted their crops in despair will shout 'Yes!' at the harvest, so those who went off with heavy hearts will come home laughing, with armloads of blessing."

Apple trees were another experiment we tried on our land this year. The owner of the local tree farm gave us advice, and we planted two flourishing trees that would bloom in the same season. We did everything by the book. We even fertilized. But guess what our harvest was this year? One measly little apple the size of a quarter.

We've been learning a lot about real life from our gardening experiments. Even when you do everything right, sometimes you still don't get the results you were hoping for. So we pray in the difficult times of life and ask for God's blessing on the next season. We trust that God is good and present, bringing new life just around the bend.

Lord, thanks for teaching me real life lessons through all the different seasons You've given me in Your creation.

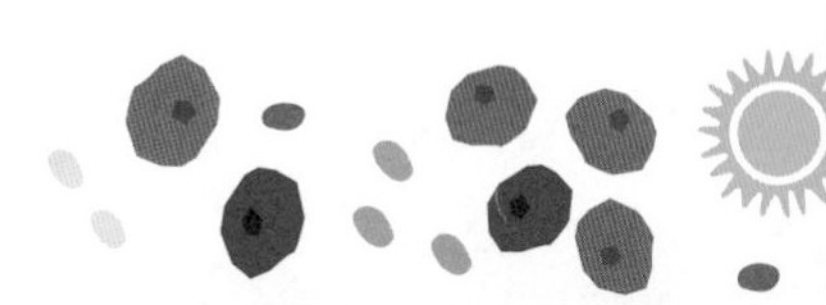

THE FRUIT OF JOY AND LOVE

The Holy Spirit produces this kind of fruit in our lives: love, joy, peace, patience, kindness, goodness, faithfulness, gentleness, and self-control. There is no law against these things!

GALATIANS 5:22–23 NLT

Did you know that joy is a fruit of the Spirit? Spiritual fruit is gathered when you allow Jesus, the Master Gardener, to plant and cultivate His Spirit in your heart. Jesus talks a lot about fruit. Take a look at this: "No branch can bear fruit by itself; it must remain in the vine. Neither can you bear fruit unless you remain in me" (John 15:4 NIV).

Remember the law of sowing and reaping? What you plant, you reap. If you plant watermelons, you can't expect to reap beans, right? The same is true in the garden of your heart. If you plant negativity, discontentment, busyness, and excess social media, should you expect the fruit of joy to grow? Nope! Not how it works.

If you've noticed that the crops in your life aren't producing good fruit, ask Jesus to start pulling out the weeds and preparing your heart for His fruits to grow instead.

Lord, I think I might need some pruning in my life. I want to grow good fruit. Please show me what weeds we need to pull so that Your love and joy can grow there instead.

MORE GARDENING

Light is sown [like seed] for the righteous and illuminates their path, and [irrepressible] joy [is spread] for the upright in heart [who delight in His favor and protection].

PSALM 97:11 AMP

This gardening thing is a pretty big deal in the Bible! God used lots of imagery in His Word so that people could easily understand what He meant. Many of His followers were farmers, and most people had at least a little garden, so the reaping and sowing messages made a lot of sense.

Today's verse contains more gardening metaphors. *The Message* says it this way: "Light-seeds are planted in the souls of God's people, joy-seeds are planted in good heart-soil."

God plants light and joy in the hearts of His people. An "irrepressible joy" is spread out like seed all over your heart.

The landscape fabric we bought for our garden controls or "represses" the weeds and smothers their growth. But the joy God plants in you is "irrepressible"! It can't be smothered if you are delighting in Jesus and remaining in Him (John 15).

What does remaining in Jesus mean to you? Talk to Jesus about this today!

Lord Jesus, I want to remain in You so that all Your good fruit will continue growing in me. Please show me what that means. I'm excited to grow "irrepressible joy"!

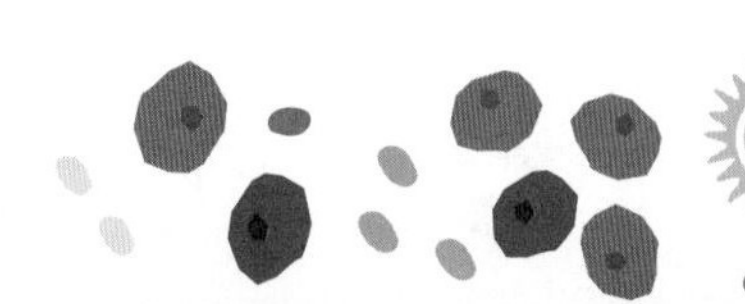

GREAT OAKS AND BEAUTY

To all who mourn in Israel, he will give a crown of beauty for ashes, a joyous blessing instead of mourning, festive praise instead of despair. In their righteousness, they will be like great oaks that the LORD has planted for his own glory.

ISAIAH 61:3 NLT

Old plantation homes in the South were known for their long lanes of trees on both sides of the road leading up to the mansion. The trees were a beautiful and glorious sight. Many of these grand homes were burnt to the ground during the Civil War, but some still stand today.

Jesus came to turn ashes into beauty and to bring joy and blessing instead of mourning and despair. Have you ever had anything in your life feel like it exploded into flames? Do you need Jesus to bring beauty to something that seems hopeless and dead? Ask Him. You are the beloved daughter of the King. You have full access to God because of Jesus. Bring everything on your heart to Him in prayer.

Lord God, You know the problems I've faced and the hard things that still bother me. My heart is a little heavy. I bring all of this to You this morning. I need Your life-giving touch. Would You turn these ugly memories into something beautiful? I trust You, Lord.

BE THE BOOK

I'm thanking you, God, from a full heart, I'm writing the book on your wonders. I'm whistling, laughing, and jumping for joy; I'm singing your song, High God.

Psalm 9:1–2 msg

Have you ever heard the saying "You are the only Bible that some people will ever read"? That means that some people you'll meet during this lifetime have never opened a Bible or gone to church. They might have heard the name of Jesus before, but only when someone took His name in vain. God put those people in your path for a reason. You can be a living, breathing example of God's Word.

Are you writing the book of God's wonders in your life? Not literally—you don't really have to *write* a book, of course. You can *be* the book!

When you live out a life of joy and thankfulness, other people are going to wonder what is different about you. They're going to want to know why you're full of joy. They'll want to know where that joy comes from! When you're ready to share the love of Jesus, that makes you a real-life walking Bible to someone else.

Lord, as I go throughout this day, remind me that people are watching and wanting to know what a real relationship with You looks like. Prepare me to share Your joy!

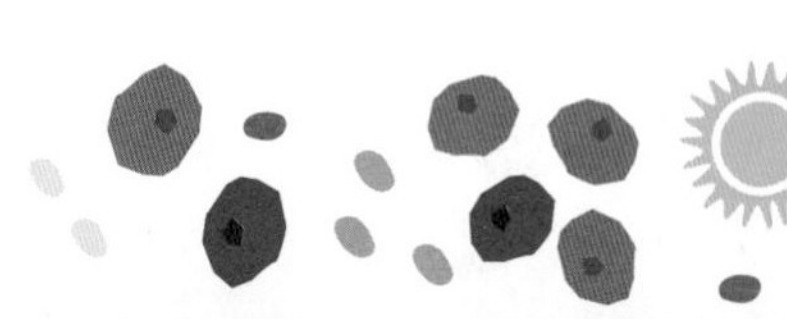

THE JOY OF MY HEART

I have taken Your testimonies as a heritage forever, for they are the joy of my heart.
Psalm 119:111 AMP

Here's an amazing truth to start your day: God doesn't treat you as your sins deserve. He is compassionate. He is gracious. Because of Jesus' work on the cross, God is not angry with you! Instead, He is abounding in love. He sees you as Jesus sees you: paid for! Your sins have been obliterated.

Check it out: "The Lord is compassionate and gracious, slow to anger, abounding in love. . . . For as high as the heavens are above the earth, so great is his love for those who fear him; as far as the east is from the west, so far has he removed our transgressions from us" (Psalm 103:8, 11–12 NIV).

No matter how many times you've messed up, God loves you and desires to be your friend. Joy comes from knowing that because of Jesus, God doesn't hold your sins against you. You are free and dearly loved. That's the good news! That's your testimony. Can you think of someone you know who needs to hear this good news today?

Lord God, You are the joy of my heart. Thank You for loving me and taking away all of my sin. Please give me the opportunity to share this joy with others.

TOTALLY HONEST

The Lord is my strength and my shield; my heart trusts in him, and he helps me. My heart leaps for joy, and with my song I praise him.

Psalm 28:7 niv

Did you know that you can be totally honest with God? You can't hide anything from Him anyway. He already knows how you feel about everything. The psalms are full of brutal honesty sometimes. But God is the safest place for you to share everything. He can shine His light on all your thoughts and feelings and help you work them out. And when you bring all of that stuff you might try to hide up to the surface, Jesus can help you get it up and out—and fill you with joy instead!

When you allow God to help you work through your issues and feelings, miraculous things happen. He turns darkness and stress and sadness into joy and singing and thanksgiving. He knows exactly what you need and how to get you from one step to the next. Say yes to God's help as you pray.

Be totally honest with God this morning. Let Him help.

My heart trusts in You, Lord. I know You can help me. Look into my heart and shine Your light there. Fill me with Your joy as we work through these feelings together.

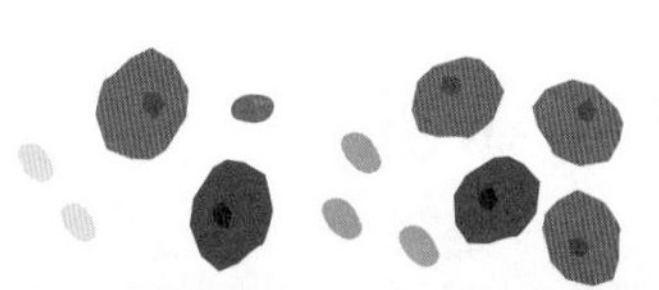

RULES GIVE JOY?

The precepts of the LORD are right, giving joy to the heart.
The commands of the LORD are radiant, giving light to the eyes.
PSALM 19:8 NIV

Wait. Rules give joy? What? Yep, that's what the Bible says! The "precepts of the LORD," His rules, give joy to the heart. How can this be? Well, God doesn't give us rules to make us unhappy. He doesn't tell us right and wrong so that we'll be miserable our entire lives. Just as wise parents set rules and good boundaries for their children, so God has given us rules to help us enjoy life better and keep us from danger.

Proverbs 3:6 (NLT) says, "Seek [God's] will in all you do, and he will show you which path to take." And Jeremiah 29:13–14 (NIV) says, "'You will seek me and find me when you seek me with all your heart. I will be found by you,' declares the LORD." When we follow God with all our hearts, He leads us and shows us where to go. This is the best way to live!

Father, I thank You for giving me rules to follow. I know You give them because You love me and want to keep me from danger. Help me respect Your rules and enjoy following them. I want my life to make You smile.

YOUR NEW NAME

We're depending on God; he's everything we need. What's more, our hearts brim with joy since we've taken for our own his holy name. Love us, God, with all you've got—that's what we're depending on.
Psalm 33:20–22 MSG

Did you know that members of a royal family don't often use or have a last name? Traditionally, their last name, or surname, comes from the land over which they preside. For example, in the United Kingdom, Princess Kate is Catherine Elizabeth Mountbatten-Windsor. She is also known as the Duchess of Cambridge and Princess of Wales. The Bible calls you royalty. Take a look for yourself:

- "But you are a chosen people, a royal priesthood, a holy nation, God's special possession." (1 Peter 2:9 NIV)
- "You will be a crown of splendor in the Lord's hand, a royal diadem in the hand of your God." (Isaiah 62:3 NIV)

So what would your new name be if you took on the land where you preside? Try it out! Add "Princess" before your first name, then say your first name, and finally add the town you live in for your last name. Hmm. . .that might make a fun sign for your door!

Even though that seems a little silly, the truth is you truly are a beloved daughter of the King of all kings. And because you depend on Him, He'll give you everything you need.

Thank You, Lord, for choosing me and calling me Your own! You fill my heart with joy, Lord, knowing that I'm Yours.

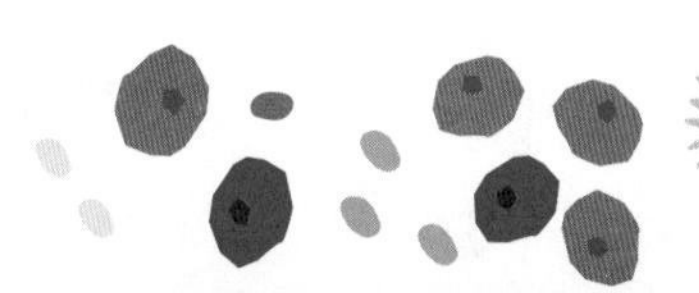

A CROWN OF JOY

The ransomed of the LORD will return and come to Zion with shouts of jubilation, and everlasting joy will be upon their heads; they will find joy and gladness, and sorrow and sighing will flee away.

ISAIAH 35:10 AMP

Isaiah was a prophet in the Old Testament. The prophets' job was to carry God's message to the people. Prophets had the difficult task of calling the people to repent and turn back to God. They brought messages of warning and judgment but also of hope.

The prophet Isaiah had all of those messages to share. In Isaiah 35, we see the promise and hope of God's kingdom after evil has been destroyed forever. This is a promise for God's children who have chosen the narrow gate in Matthew 7:13–14 (NIV): "Enter through the narrow gate. For wide is the gate and broad is the road that leads to destruction, and many enter through it. But small is the gate and narrow the road that leads to life, and only a few find it."

How do you find it? Through Jesus. He is the way, the truth, and the life (John 14:6). Follow Him all the way to the beautiful kingdom where everlasting joy will be your crown!

Jesus, thanks for opening the door for me that leads to life and joy! I will follow You!

SHARE JOY AND GRIEF

Rejoice with those who rejoice [sharing others' joy], and weep with those who weep [sharing others' grief].
ROMANS 12:15 AMP

Does God care about the things that make you sad? Yes. Psalm 56:8 (NLT) says, "You keep track of all my sorrows. You have collected all my tears in your bottle. You have recorded each one in your book."

How does knowing that Jesus has a record of every tear you've ever cried make you feel?

One of Jesus' nicknames is "Man of Sorrows" because He was rejected by people (even some of His own friends), and He was very familiar with pain and suffering. Whatever you're going through, Jesus understands because He's been there.

Jesus also wants to share in your happiness. He's a God of love, and He wants to be included in all the things you're excited about. He delights in you.

And God wants you to share in the joys and sorrows of your friends and family too. Pray for and with the people you love who are hurting. Celebrate with those who are celebrating. Be there for your friends and family.

Thanks for always being with me, Lord. I'm never alone! Help me to reach out to my family and friends in good times and bad so they know they're not alone either.

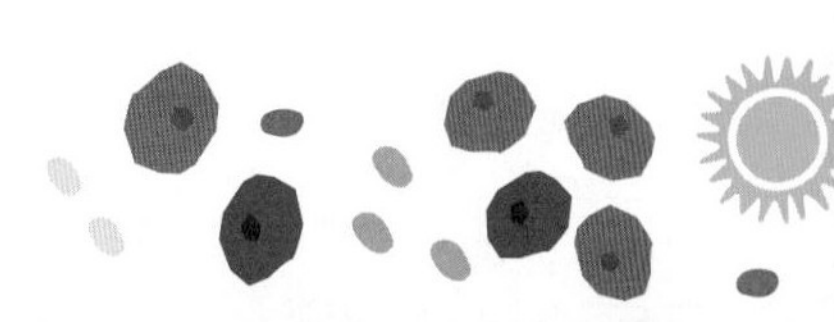

ETERNAL WEALTH

Why is everyone hungry for more? "More, more," they say. "More, more." I have God's more-than-enough, more joy in one ordinary day than they get in all their shopping sprees. At day's end I'm ready for sound sleep, for you, God, have put my life back together.

Psalm 4:6–8 MSG

Wall Street is an area of New York City known for being the home of the New York Stock Exchange. Research has been done on Wall Street employees and their stressful jobs. Many financial employees struggle with depression and fear. They are often in the news. Sadly, many have ended their own lives—or have seriously considered it. When you work in finance, you quickly discover that when you mess with a person's money, you find out what's really in that person's heart.

The Bible cautions us that the love of money will destroy you. The world idolizes money: once you have it, you can never have enough.

But God—who owns everything, by the way—offers us another way. When you lay down your idols and let Him be the center of your life, He'll give you more joy than money could ever buy.

Lord, I like earning money, and I know that's okay. Please help me to have a healthy view of money and to always submit my financial plans to You first. You are the source of eternal wealth.

THE LIFE MAP OF GOD

The revelation of God is whole and pulls our lives together.
The signposts of God are clear and point out the right road.
The life-maps of God are right, showing the way to joy.
Psalm 19:7 MSG

Do you remember making maps in grade school? The teacher gave you a list of requirements: the compass, the key, some rivers and mountains, roads, signs, and so on. You had to make sure that every symbol on your map was located in the key so that the person reading the map could figure out what the symbol meant. If you forgot even one symbol, no one would understand your map.

Thankfully, God never forgets a thing. He sees you. He's given you a road map in His Word, and all the signs are pointing to your destination. The truly amazing thing is that you aren't reading that life map alone. You have God's Spirit inside you, pointing the way. And Jesus is taking your hand, walking with you every step of the way. X marks the spot to joy!

Jesus, I love picturing You in my prayers, taking my hand and walking with me on this journey of life. With Your Spirit inside me, I'm in for a joyful adventure all the way home!

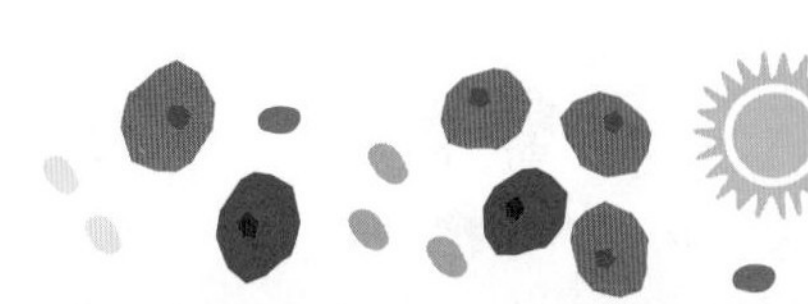

JOY IN THE TRIALS

Consider it nothing but joy, my brothers and sisters, whenever you fall into various trials. Be assured that the testing of your faith [through experience] produces endurance [leading to spiritual maturity, and inner peace].

JAMES 1:2–3 AMP

Have you ever had something upsetting or embarrassing happen to you and you shook it off, pretending everything was okay, when really you were hurting inside, and it affected everything that happened after that?

When you read in James 1 to "count it all joy" when something bad happens, it may seem like that's what the Bible is saying, but—hear me on this—it's not. God doesn't want you to bury your feelings and pretend like nothing is wrong. That would be a form of lying.

Instead, God wants you to see things from a heavenly perspective. He wants you to come to Him first with all of your thoughts and feelings. Tell Him exactly how it makes you feel! He'll help you process your feelings. And then you'll be able to look at the hard stuff more positively, knowing that, eventually, God promises everything will work out all right (Romans 8:28!).

I know You're doing good things in my heart, Lord. I know You care about my thoughts and feelings. Please help me keep my eyes on You during hard times. I trust You, Lord.

WHEN YOU'RE FRESH OUT OF JOY

Restore to me the joy of your salvation and grant me a willing spirit, to sustain me.
PSALM 51:12 NIV

Have you ever felt completely worn out? So tired of drama that you just want to go away and hide for a while? Or maybe your season of change and hard times is lasting a little too long and you simply can't find any rest right now. Sometimes those feelings can cause us to lose the joy of our faith.

When we lose our joy for loving and serving God, we also lose our strength. Remember Nehemiah 8:10? The Bible says that the joy of the Lord *is* our strength! So when we can't find joy in our relationship with God, we run out of strength completely. Yikes!

What can you do about it? Come to Jesus. Get close. Tell Him what's on your heart. Maybe write it all down in a journal. Ask God to supernaturally fill you with His joy once again. God can give you His strength to live life with joy, even in a long and difficult season.

Father, will You please fill me with Your joy again? I'm afraid I may have lost it. Please give me Your strength and put a new song of joy in my heart.

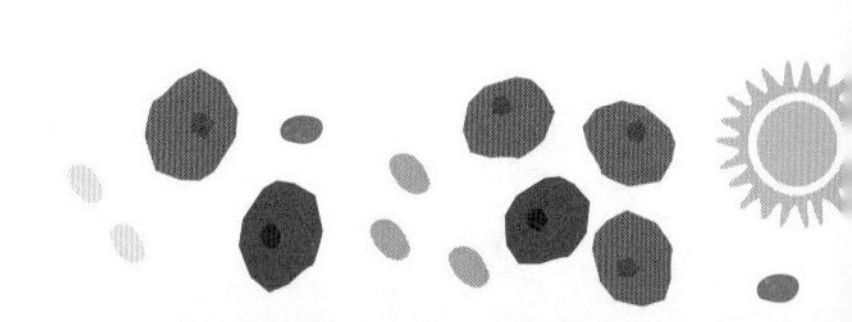

SO MUCH JOY

"So with you: Now is your time of grief, but I will see you again and you will rejoice, and no one will take away your joy."
John 16:22 NIV

We've talked a lot about joy over the last few weeks. The Bible has a lot to say about joy! Here's a few more verses to ponder before we move on:

- "You have turned my mourning into joyful dancing. You have taken away my clothes of mourning and clothed me with joy, that I might sing praises to you and not be silent. O Lord my God, I will give you thanks forever!" (Psalm 30:11–12 NLT)
- "When anxiety was great within me, your consolation brought me joy." (Psalm 94:19 NIV)
- "In [God] our heart rejoices, because we trust [lean on, rely on, and are confident] in His holy name." (Psalm 33:21 AMP)

The bottom line? Joy is yours! It's part of your inheritance as a daughter of the King! When you "trust, lean on, rely on, and are confident in" Jesus, joy is yours. It's right around the corner. Be on the lookout because joy is coming!

Jesus, Your closeness fills me with joy! I trust Your promises. No matter what I have going on, Your presence brings joy. I'm thankful I have an eternity with You to look forward to.

YOU BELONG

You are the body of Christ, and each one of you is a part of it.
1 Corinthians 12:27 NIV

Have you ever walked into a room at church or school or someplace where there were a lot of kids your age and you instantly felt like you didn't belong? I think that's a common feeling when you're in a place where you don't know many people. But even adults still struggle with this when they're visiting different places—even at church!

Here's the thing: when you're around other Christians, you belong because God says you do. He made you an important part of the body—His body—the body of Christ! If you're moving to a new town or getting involved at a new church for the first time, it's okay to be shy at first. That's normal. You can take your time getting to know new people, making friends, and sharing your gifts and talents with others. But don't be intimidated! God made you a special part of His body, and He has a good place for you to be exactly who He created you to be. We're going to talk more about that in the coming weeks.

Father, thanks for reminding me that I belong. I trust You to show me the place I'm needed and where I'm supposed to be.

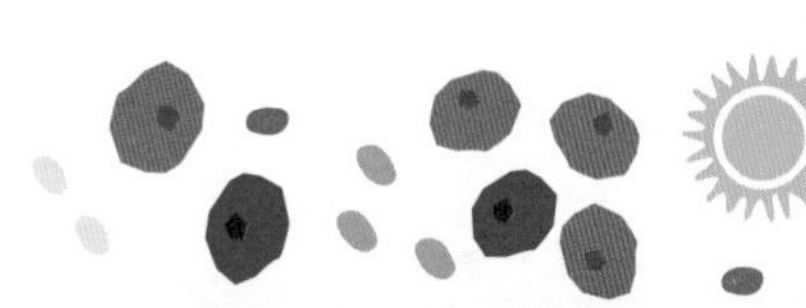

RIGHT WHERE GOD WANTS YOU

I want you to think about how all this makes you more significant, not less. A body isn't just a single part blown up into something huge. It's all the different-but-similar parts arranged and functioning together. . . . If Ear said, "I'm not beautiful like Eye, transparent and expressive; I don't deserve a place on the head," would you want to remove it from the body? . . . As it is, we see that God has carefully placed each part of the body right where he wanted it.
1 CORINTHIANS 12:14–18 MSG

God has special plans and purposes for you in His body. Think about your own body for a moment. Your toes have a very different function than your heart, right? Your toes might not seem that important when compared to the heart, but if you research why your body needs its toes, you'll see that they are very important! They help you balance and run fast. And what girl doesn't love her toes painted cute when sporting summer flip-flops?

You might not think that your gifts and talents contribute much in the body of Christ, but that's simply not true. You have an important part to play, and God has placed you right where He wants you.

Lord, thank You for showing me that I am an important part of Your body.

CREATED IN GOD'S IMAGE

God created human beings in his own image. In the image of God he created them; male and female he created them. . . . Then God looked over all he had made, and he saw that it was very good!
GENESIS 1:27, 31 NLT

God is the great Creator of all things. And He set eternity right there in your heart. Ecclesiastes 3:11 (NIV) tells us, "He has made everything beautiful in its time. He has also set eternity in the human heart; yet no one can fathom what God has done from beginning to end."

God is the master artist, and you are His masterpiece. He signed His name on your life and put His Spirit in your heart.

Anne Shirley, the lovable, talkative, redheaded character created by Lucy Maud Montgomery, said that someone told her "God made my hair red on purpose, and I've never cared about him since." But she learned to say her prayers, nonetheless.

God did make you the way you are on purpose. So instead of getting upset about your body shape or the color of your hair, trust that God designed you the way you are on purpose. Ask Him to help you see yourself the way He does—with eyes of love.

Lord, help me accept myself as I am—
created in Your image on purpose.

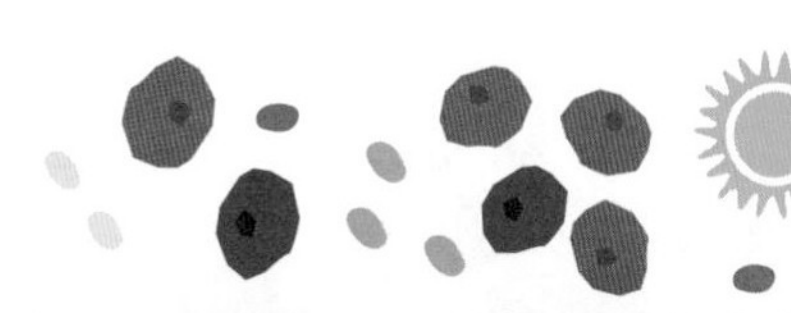

CREATED TO CREATE

In him all things were created: things in heaven and on earth, visible and invisible, whether thrones or powers or rulers or authorities; all things have been created through him and for him.

Colossians 1:16 NIV

I listened to a pastor describe a bunch of grade-schoolers who were surveyed about their art abilities. When asked how many artists were in the room, every kindergartener raised their hand. Most first-graders raised their hand. Many second-graders lifted a hand. But by the third grade, fewer kids thought they were artist material. Only a few brave souls in the fifth grade believed they were artists.

As kids grow and get feedback from others, their confidence in their abilities tends to reflect what other people say about them. But you were created to create. When you think up something creative, you are a reflection of God. When you design something or transform your room or take a really cool picture, that's a trait that comes from the heart of God.

You don't have to be an amazing artist to be creative. Every time you come up with a new idea, you're doing what God created you to do.

Lord, thanks for creating me with an imagination. Help me use my creative ideas to give You glory and reflect who You are.

BEAUTIFULLY FUNCTIONAL

Yet, O LORD, You are our Father; we are the clay, and You our Potter, and we all are the work of Your hand.

ISAIAH 64:8 AMP

In middle school art class, we learned how to make a lump of clay into something useful. We could choose a mug or a bowl or a vase—something relatively simple. The teacher taught us how to mold the clay on the spinning wheel. It was a messy task, but the clay eventually resembled something. Then we let it dry out, fired it in a kiln, glazed it, and fired it again. The results varied. Some creations looked okay, others not so much. Yet we were all proud that we made something useful with our own hands.

One pottery-making website insists that there are no mistakes in pottery while you're in the creative stage. You get as many do-overs as you want before you let the clay dry. Simply smoosh that clay together and start again.

God is continually crafting us into a beautiful masterpiece too. As we yield to His hands, He turns us into something functional and beautiful that brings glory and honor to Him.

Lord, I yield my life to Your creative hands. Make me into something useful that brings You glory.

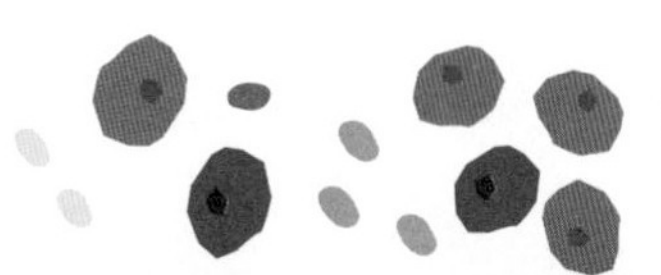

WHY JESUS CAME

The Spirit of the Sovereign Lord is upon me, for the Lord has anointed me to bring good news to the poor. He has sent me to comfort the brokenhearted and to proclaim that captives will be released and prisoners will be freed. He has sent me to tell those who mourn that the time of the Lord's favor has come, and with it, the day of God's anger against their enemies.

Isaiah 61:1–2 NLT

Isaiah prophesied these words in the Old Testament hundreds and hundreds of years before Jesus was born. And in Luke 4:16–21 (NIV), we see Jesus enter the synagogue, stand up, and read Isaiah's words. He began by saying, "The Spirit of the Lord is on me," and ended with "to proclaim the year of the Lord's favor." Then He added something utterly amazing: "Today this scripture is fulfilled in your hearing."

Jesus was publicly announcing why He had come. He comes to you just the same. He has great news for you! He comes to comfort you and set you free from sin and shame. Are you hurting or feeling imprisoned by anything or anyone right now? Invite Jesus in to break the chains and set you free.

Thank You, Jesus, for giving me hope and bringing healing and wholeness to my heart.

JESUS CAME TO BRING COMFORT

Praise be to the God and Father of our Lord Jesus Christ, the Father of compassion and the God of all comfort, who comforts us in all our troubles, so that we can comfort those in any trouble with the comfort we ourselves receive from God.

2 Corinthians 1:3–4 niv

Jesus came for you in so many ways. God's Word tells us that Jesus came to comfort those with broken hearts. Are you hurting about something today? Bring it before Jesus. Do you have a friend or family member with a broken heart? Pray for them to find comfort in Christ alone.

When you know that you belong because God says you do, you can comfort others with the same comfort you have received from God. God uses everything you've ever gone through. Difficult things that you've endured with the help of Jesus can be used to comfort friends going through the same kind of thing. Nothing is wasted.

Allow Jesus to comfort all the places in your heart that need an extra snuggle. Then go out and share the comfort of Jesus with the people He puts on your path who need comfort too.

Jesus, I'm thankful for the ways You comfort me. Help me be on the lookout for those around me who need that same kind of comfort.

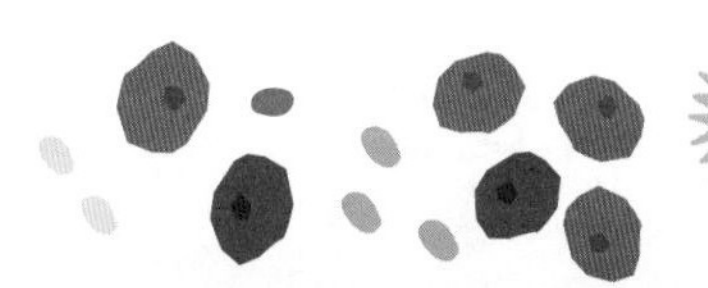

FREEDOM ON THE JOURNEY

Christ has truly set us free. Now make sure that you stay free, and don't get tied up again in slavery to the law.
GALATIANS 5:1 NLT

Christians have been making up lists of dos and don'ts for centuries. Jesus came to complete that list and bring freedom. That doesn't mean you're free to be selfish and do whatever you want. It means you don't have to follow a bunch of rules that people made up to get to heaven.

A friend of mine was very excited about going to church and finding Jesus for the first time. She was joyful and eager to go to church. A few months later, I saw her again, and she was down and discouraged. I asked her what was wrong, and she said, "There's just so much to learn!"

Well-meaning church people were trying to give her a list of things to do to live the Christian life. My friend felt weighed down by those rules and was losing the joy she found in Christ.

Be careful not to set your Christian expectations on others. Each of us is on a journey with Jesus that will look different depending on God's specific will for us.

Jesus, thank You for making me truly free! Please help me have grace and understanding for other people on their individual journeys with You.

SET FREE TO SERVE

You have been called to live in freedom, my brothers and sisters. But don't use your freedom to satisfy your sinful nature. Instead, use your freedom to serve one another in love.

GALATIANS 5:13 NLT

Yesterday we talked about having freedom in Christ. We each have an individual journey with Jesus that will look different from other people's experiences. We've been called to live in that freedom. But again, that doesn't mean we're free to be selfish. That's not why Jesus came. Jesus said in Matthew 20:28 (NLT), "The Son of Man came not to be served but to serve others and to give his life as a ransom for many."

Serving others brings great joy. When we submit our hearts and lives to Jesus, He fills us with His Spirit and gives us strength and a desire to do His will. Our love for Him bubbles up into service and love for others. This is Christianity in action.

If you're feeling weighed down by Christian rules and guilt-induced service, that's not from Jesus. That's not the Spirit-filled life He has for you. If you're struggling in this area, ask Jesus to give you clear direction. He wants you set free to serve out of love.

Lord, please give me a heart to serve out of my love for You!

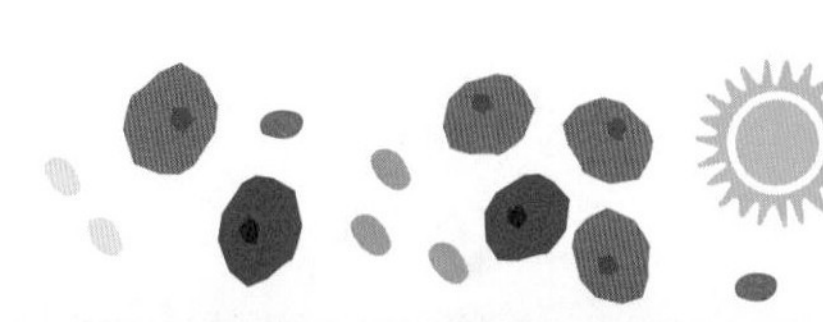

PRAYING FOR YOUR BROTHERS AND SISTERS

Finally, believers, rejoice! Be made complete [be what you should be], be comforted, be like-minded, live in peace [enjoy the spiritual well-being experienced by believers who walk closely with God]; and the God of love and peace [the source of lovingkindness] will be with you.

2 CORINTHIANS 13:11 AMP

You belong to the body of Christ, and fellow believers are your brothers and sisters in Christ. That makes you part of a huge worldwide family! Ephesians 6:18 (NLT) says, "Pray in the Spirit at all times and on every occasion. Stay alert and be persistent in your prayers for all believers everywhere."

God wants us to support and pray for one another as brothers and sisters. Does your church support any missionaries? Pray for them, even if you don't know their names. In Ephesians 6:19 (NIV), Paul wrote, "Pray also for me, that whenever I speak, words may be given me so that I will fearlessly make known the mystery of the gospel." Pray for all missionaries that they would share the love of Jesus without fear.

Pray also for your church and any ministry teams you belong to. Pray for truth, love, peace, and joy to be known and felt at your church.

Lord, I lift up my brothers and sisters all around the world. Help us to live authentic and loving lives based on the truth of Your Word.

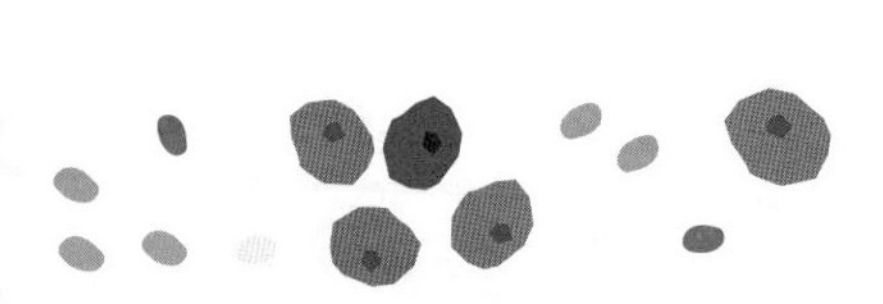

GOD MADE YOU TO BELONG

Then the Lord God said, "It is not good for the man to be alone. I will make a helper who is just right for him."
Genesis 2:18 NLT

Remember back at the beginning of creation? God had finished making everything, and then He brought each kind of animal to Adam so that Adam could name them. Yeah, it might have been Adam who decided a yak should have a weird name like that (or it could have been the explorer who came upon the beast centuries later, since Adam probably didn't write down any animal names). There are a lot of animals! You or I would probably just start putting letters together to make a name after a day full of naming everything: *Let's see—hippopotamus, Bornean orangutan, uh...bat, ox...*

Well, after God and Adam went through all the animals, none of them was good enough to be Adam's helper. That's right, not even Fido—"man's best friend." God had something else in mind. He wanted people to help one another. To belong to one another. To inspire and encourage one other. You were not meant to travel the world alone. You need more than a furry buddy to survive. God put you in a family and gave you the friends you have for a reason.

Lord, thanks for creating me and placing me in a family to belong!

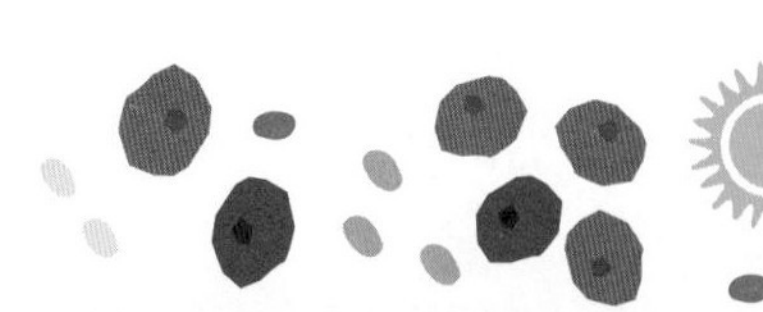

THE GIFT OF FRIENDSHIP

By yourself you're unprotected. With a friend you can face the worst. Can you round up a third? A three-stranded rope isn't easily snapped.

Ecclesiastes 4:12 MSG

In the Lord of the Rings books and movies, there are three warriors—Aragorn, Legolas, and Gimli—who come to one another's aid many times throughout the story. At first, they know next to nothing about one another, but as time passes during their mutual quest, they become fast friends and companions. They rely on one another for help. They have one another's backs. They keep one another from near death multiple times because they care about one another.

Good friends are a gift in this life. And your friendships are important to God. If you're struggling to find good friends at this point in your life, ask God for help. Seek Him in your friendships and listen as He leads you toward people who will encourage you. If you have that already, thank God for His gift of friendship! Pray for your friends and seek to encourage them in their walk with Jesus.

Lord, I bring my friendships to You this morning. I want to honor You in all of my relationships. Help me to be a good friend and look out for the people You've put in my life. Thanks for the special gift of friendship.

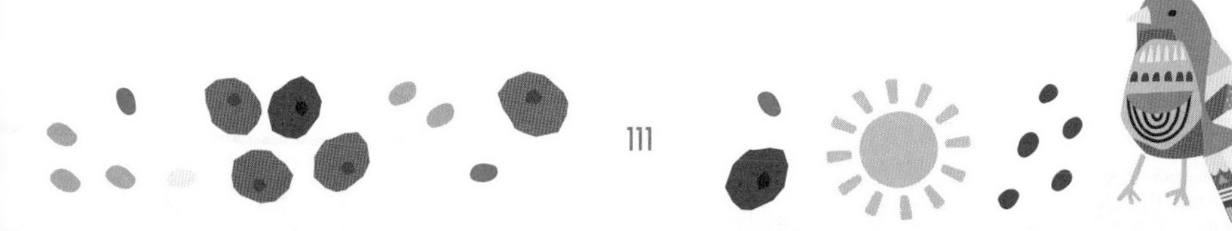

HELLOS AND GOODBYES

Friends come and friends go, but a true friend sticks by you like family.
PROVERBS 18:24 MSG

Life is full of hellos and goodbyes. Many people come in and out of our life during different seasons. When you're in gymnastics as a ten-year-old, you have friends you only see there. Then when you're twelve, you might switch to volleyball and have a totally new set of friends.

As you grow and change, you have new and different friends, depending on where you live and what activities you're involved in. But sometimes you find a friend at church or school who is always there. They feel more like a sister than a friend.

These kinds of friends are blessings from God. The Bible says that God sets the lonely in families (Psalm 68:6). He brings good friends into our lives to become our sisters in Christ, forming a new family as part of the body of Christ. God is good like that. He provides everything you'll ever need.

So even though you'll face some hellos and goodbyes in this life, God will bring the right people into your life at the right time. It's great to be a part of the family of God!

Lord, You care so much about me, bringing me good friends and placing me in Your family. Thank You!

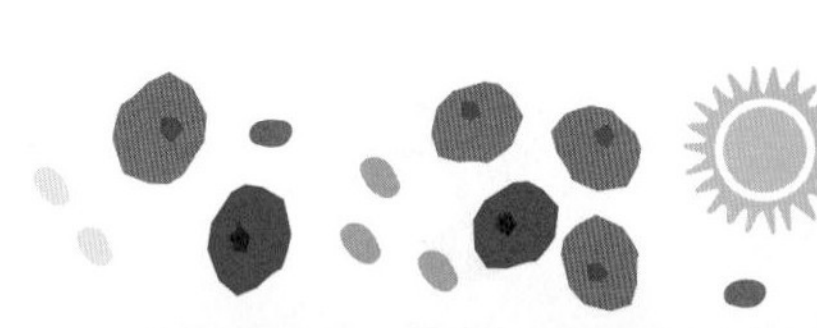

THE BUDDY SYSTEM

Two people are better off than one, for they can help each other succeed. If one person falls, the other can reach out and help. But someone who falls alone is in real trouble.
ECCLESIASTES 4:9–10 NLT

Mom said it. Your teacher said it. Your youth pastor said it: "Don't go alone. Take a buddy with you!"

You have to admit, it's wise advice. Even police officers have partners. There is always safety in numbers. Not only is this wise advice from parents and teachers, but it's also wise advice from God's Word.

This advice isn't just about going somewhere safely in pairs like heading to the girls' bathroom. This is also talking about not being a loner. It's important to let others in and to share your thoughts and feelings with others. Trying to do everything on your own without ever asking for advice, help, or prayer isn't a good thing. God meant for us to help and encourage one another.

How are you doing with letting others into your world? Are you good at asking for advice or prayer from people you trust? Talk to God about this. Ask Him to open doors for good and safe people to be a part of your life.

Lord, please bring some safe people into my life who I can trust for advice and encouragement.

FRIENDS MATTER

Do not be deceived: "Bad company corrupts good morals."
1 Corinthians 15:33 AMP

The Bible has some things to say about who you shouldn't be friends with. Does that surprise you? Doesn't the Bible say we're supposed to love everybody?

Yes, we're supposed to show God's love to others, but who you choose to spend most of your time with is not the same thing. The people you let speak into your life are very important to God. He cares about who you choose as your best friends.

Check it out:

- "He who walks [as a companion] with wise men will be wise, but the companions of [conceited, dull-witted] fools [are fools themselves and] will experience harm." (Proverbs 13:20 AMP)
- "Don't befriend angry people or associate with hot-tempered people, or you will learn to be like them and endanger your soul." (Proverbs 22:24–25 NLT)
- "But I *am* saying that you shouldn't act as if everything is just fine when a friend who claims to be a Christian is promiscuous or crooked, is flip with God or rude to friends, gets drunk or becomes greedy and predatory. You can't just go along with this, treating it as acceptable behavior." (1 Corinthians 5:12 MSG)

Christian friends are a necessity on life's journey. And it's very important to choose them wisely!

Lord, I'm hearing You. My friend choices matter to You. Help me choose wisely!

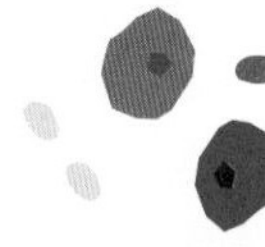
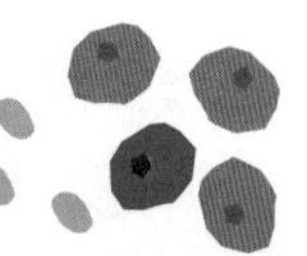

NO ONE LEFT BEHIND

So speak encouraging words to one another. Build up hope so you'll all be together in this, no one left out, no one left behind. I know you're already doing this; just keep on doing it.

1 THESSALONIANS 5:11 MSG

The military has had a motto for hundreds of years that says, "No man left behind." They want to make sure that every person in their troop is accounted for at the end of the mission or battle.

It's so easy to want to be first. To be the leader. To get in the front of the line. But a good leader makes sure that everyone is accounted for.

Look around. Look for the kids that look lonely or left out. Treat them the way you would want to be treated if you were in their shoes. Strike up a conversation. Ask them how their day is or how they are feeling.

It can be hard and embarrassing to talk to shy people, but God can give you His strength and wisdom to reach out. Look around and help someone else feel like they belong too.

Lord, I admit I get really caught up in the fun my friends and I are having. Help me be on the lookout for people who may feel left behind. Please give me courage to help.

GOOD ADVICE

Oil and perfume make the heart glad; so does the sweetness of a friend's counsel that comes from the heart.
PROVERBS 27:9 AMP

Teenagers need advice. You have so many plans and dreams and hopes for your life. You have so many directions to choose from and decisions to make. Getting wise counsel is a good thing. Here are a few things the Bible has to say about that:

- "Refuse good advice and watch your plans fail; take good counsel and watch them succeed." (Proverbs 15:22 MSG)
- "Take good counsel and accept correction—that's the way to live wisely and well." (Proverbs 19:20 MSG)
- "But the wisdom from above is first of all pure. It is also peace loving, gentle at all times, and willing to yield to others. It is full of mercy and the fruit of good deeds. It shows no favoritism and is always sincere." (James 3:17 NLT)

As a child of God, belonging to His family, you have access to all of God's resources and wisdom. Tap into the wisdom He offers you through other safe and loving believers. Your life will go more smoothly then.

Lord, help me be humble and wise enough to seek good advice from Your people. Show me the areas in my life where I need more direction. Send the right people to help.

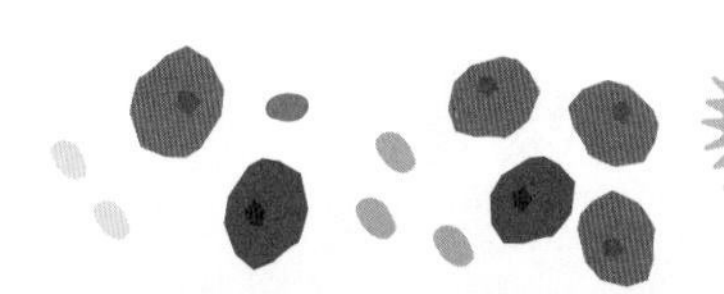

GOSSIP SEPARATES

A troublemaker plants seeds of strife;
gossip separates the best of friends.
Proverbs 16:28 NLT

Families often make light of gossip and even encourage it under the guise of "just wanting to help." But we all know that gossip hurts. No one likes to walk into a room only to hear "the hush" and realize they were the topic of discussion. Proverbs 18:7–8 (NIV) says, "The mouths of fools are their undoing, and their lips are a snare to their very lives. The words of a gossip are like choice morsels; they go down to the inmost parts." If you want to encourage belonging with your friends, don't gossip.

Remember this: "You can tell more about a person by what he says about others than you can by what others say about him" (Leo Aikman). If Kerry is going to say bad things about Jesse, she is likely to say bad things about you too.

And if you're always worried about what other people are saying about you behind your back, maybe *you* are saying a little too much about everyone else! Don't let your mouth be your undoing. Ask the Lord to help you keep a tight rein on your tongue (James 1:26).

Lord, I repent of gossiping. I need Your help to say good and encouraging things instead of talking about people behind their backs.

TIME FOR CHURCH

Let us think of ways to motivate one another to acts of love and good works. And let us not neglect our meeting together, as some people do, but encourage one another, especially now that the day of his return is drawing near.

HEBREWS 10:24–25 NLT

What's your church like? Is it a small country church where you sing hymns and everyone feels like family? Is it a large church with a band and you meet in small groups to get to know others? Whatever kind of church your family has chosen, church is important. The Bible tells us to get together with other believers regularly. Why? Because the people you hang around most affect how you act and think. Fellow believers will help remind you that you're a child of the King and that Jesus is coming again soon! They will pray for you and offer wise advice from God's Word. Worshipping together is uplifting and powerful.

If you're in a work or school environment without a lot of other believers, maintaining a positive and Christlike attitude can be difficult. So get to church, my friend! It's meant to help.

Thanks for my church, Lord. I pray for my pastors and leaders that You would protect them and give them wisdom to lead and shepherd by listening for Your voice.

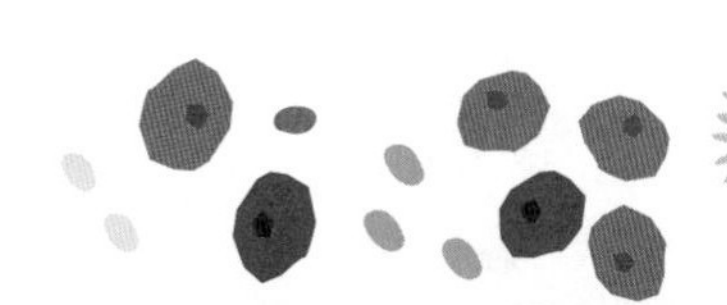

TAKING CARE OF THE BODY

Most important of all, continue to show deep love for each other, for love covers a multitude of sins. Cheerfully share your home with those who need a meal or a place to stay. God has given each of you a gift from his great variety of spiritual gifts. Use them well to serve one another.

1 PETER 4:8–10 NLT

You've learned how to take good care of your own body, right? You make sure you eat the right foods with the occasional treat. You're pretty good at doing your own hair and cleaning your teeth. You trim your nails when needed and add some pretty polish to top off your look.

God wants us to take care of the body of Christ too. Taking care of our own bodies and caring for the body of Christ have a lot of parallels. If you know that your brothers and sisters in Christ need something, see how you can help. Share meals. Bless them with some of your gifts and talents. Ask God to help you reach out in loving care to His body. There are a lot of needs around you, and God equips His family to meet those needs when everyone is willing to share.

Lord, please open my eyes so I can see and help meet the needs around me.

LET IT GO

Love prospers when a fault is forgiven, but dwelling on it separates close friends.
PROVERBS 17:9 NLT

Let it go! Can you even hear those words without belting out the catchy song? The words might have been made popular by a cartoon princess, but the idea of letting things go comes from the Bible.

Matthew 11:30 (MSG) says, "Learn the unforced rhythms of grace. I won't lay anything heavy or ill-fitting on you. Keep company with me and you'll learn to live freely and lightly."

Hanging on to old hurts isn't good for friendships, and it's not good for your heart either. When a friend or family member hurts you, intentionally or not, ask God for the courage to help you talk to them about it. Try to work things out, offer forgiveness, and then let it go.

When you let things go, it doesn't mean you're sweeping things under the rug; it means you're giving your hurts to Jesus and allowing Him to work in the situation. You can trust that He'll lead you forward as you learn to live freely and lightly.

Lord, I really love the idea of living freely and lightly. Help me learn to let go of things that weigh me down. Help me love others well and learn to forgive wholeheartedly.

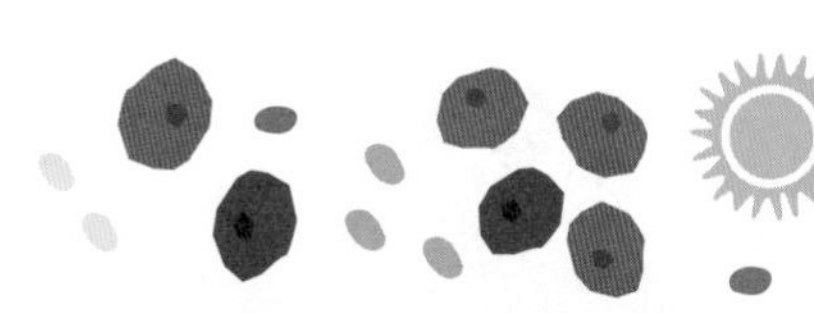

THE GOLDEN RULE

"Do to others as you would have them do to you."
Luke 6:31 NIV

You know the Golden Rule. Even people in the secular world and public schools talk about this ancient rule.

Luke 6:31–33 (MSG) says it this way: "Here is a simple rule of thumb for behavior: Ask yourself what you want people to do for you, then grab the initiative and do it for them! If you only love the lovable, do you expect a pat on the back? Run-of-the-mill sinners do that. If you only help those who help you, do you expect a medal?"

Interesting questions, right? When siblings get into arguments at home, it can sometimes sound like this: "Well, he took my sandwich so I'm going to take his cookie."

And when you get older, the sibling fight can sound like this: "She went ten minutes over on screen time, so I'm not giving this back to her until I get my extra time."

Does any of that sound familiar? The problem is that this is exactly the opposite of what Jesus says. Instead of saying, "Well, she did this, so I'm going to do it too," ask Jesus to remind you that you don't like being treated that way and then do the opposite.

Jesus, please help me do better at living out the Golden Rule, especially with my family!

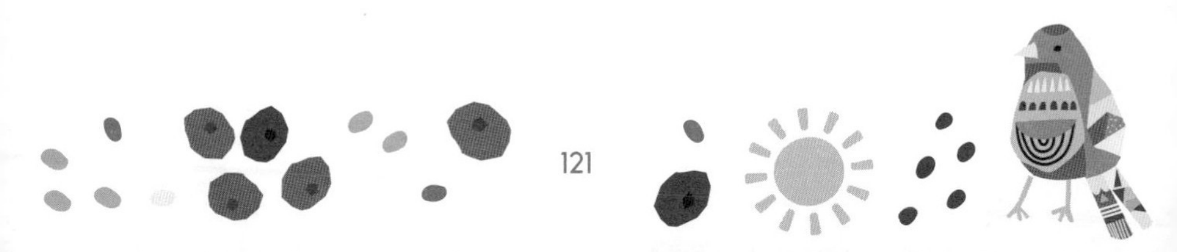

YOUR FAMILY AT HOME

"Honor your father and mother. Then you will live a long, full life in the land the LORD your God is giving you."
EXODUS 20:12 NLT

God placed you in a family. It may not resemble other families, and that's okay. But you do have some authority figures in your life who God placed there for a reason. God designed families to help nurture you, teach you about God, and prepare you to be a responsible adult.

Sadly, not all families work this way. The stats on child abuse in the United States are staggering. Over three million cases of child abuse are reported every year, and many more go unreported, especially emotional abuse and neglect cases.

If you live in a happy home, thank God and thank your parents. This is a huge blessing not to be taken for granted. If you feel safe and free in your family, you are blessed! Pray for the abused children in your area to find help and healing. Talk to your parents about how your family might get involved in helping at-risk families in your area.

Lord, I'm thankful that I'm safe and free and loved! Give me the desire to help others who don't have what I've been given. Show my family ways to help.

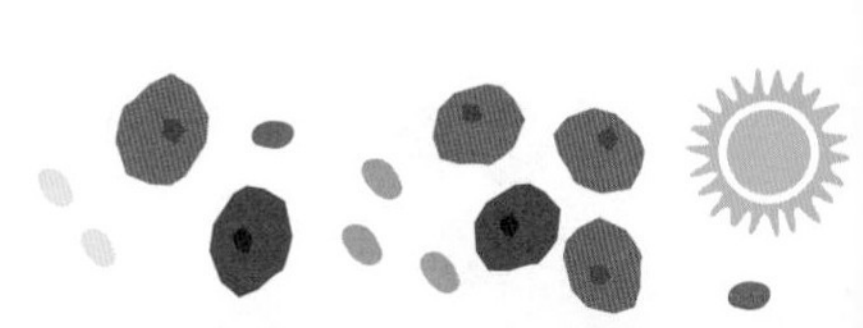

THE BLESSING OF OBEDIENCE

Children, obey your parents [as God's representatives] in all things, for this [attitude of respect and obedience] is well-pleasing to the Lord [and will bring you God's promised blessings].
COLOSSIANS 3:20 AMP

The word *obey* can be a hard pill to swallow. Strong-willed children struggle. Teenagers cringe at the very thought. Many adults simply balk at the idea of obeying anyone else. If you've been to a wedding lately, you've likely heard the traditional marriage vow of "love, honor, and obey" replaced with modern language.

But God has set up families so that children obey their parents as parents and families obey God. Learning obedience as children sets us up for a lifetime of blessing as we obey God.

How can you obey your parents with a happy heart this week? Pray for God to help you honor your parents and their position of authority in your life. Think of ways to bless your parents today.

If your parents haven't made a commitment to follow Jesus, pray for them. Many times it's the faith of a child that can cause a hardened heart to soften toward Christ and His love.

Lord, I'm thankful for my parents. Help me obey and honor them. Show me ways to bless them today.

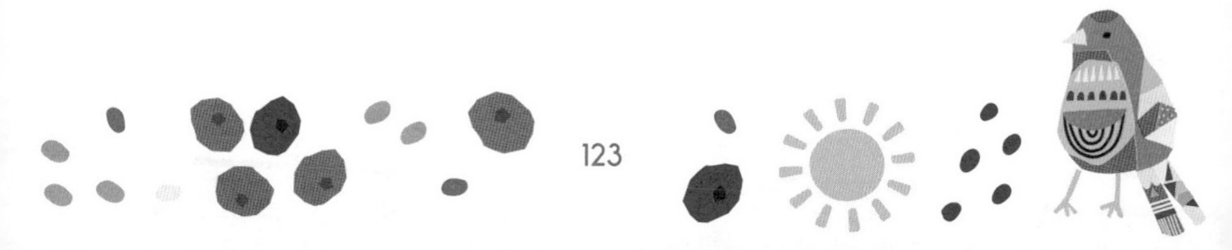

MEAT LOAF, MAC AND CHEESE, AND SPAGHETTI

Better is a dinner of vegetables and herbs where love is present than a fattened ox served with hatred.
PROVERBS 15:17 AMP

Royal families throughout history have enjoyed the best of the best of everything: food, drink, clothing, jewels. Egyptian royalty was known for having their family members killed so they could make their way to the throne. Imagine having everything you ever wanted yet not being able to sleep peacefully for fear your sister or brother might have you killed in your sleep!

Today's proverb is a reminder that being loved is always better than wealth. A family I knew growing up lived on very little but a tiny salary and the charity of others in their small congregation, and they were the happiest and most loving people you could ever meet.

As you eat your spaghetti or mac and cheese tonight, be thankful for the family God has given you. Consider writing each family member a little note letting them know how thankful you are. Thank Mom or Dad for cooking the meal. Be thankful for the love you share.

Lord, thanks for my family. We may not have much, but I'm really thankful for the kindness and love we share.

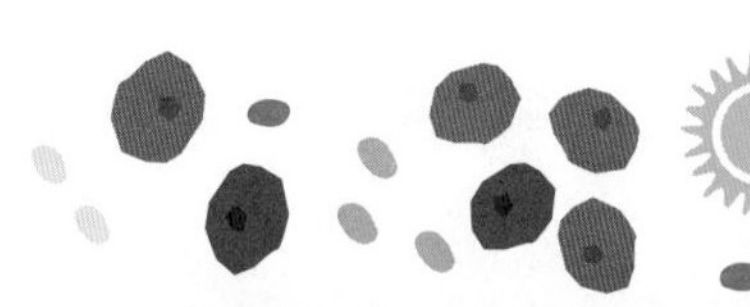

SIBLINGS AND FRIENDS

Do not rebuke an older man harshly, but exhort him as if he were your father. Treat younger men as brothers, older women as mothers, and younger women as sisters, with absolute purity.

1 Timothy 5:1–2 NIV

Timothy was a young pastor, and Paul was writing letters to instruct him on how to lead his church successfully. Paul gave him advice on how to treat his brothers and sisters in Christ. This is good advice for us today: respect your elders and treat younger kids like well-loved siblings. There is a trend today in books and movies for siblings to treat one another with disrespect. The "annoying little brother" and the "bratty big sister" are common themes. This is not how God wants us to view and treat our siblings.

Sure, there are times when siblings need their space. But God gave you siblings as built-in friends. You learn how to have relationships in a family. Your siblings become your best friends for life. Treat them well now, even if they get on your nerves sometimes, so that you can enjoy a good friendship for a lifetime.

Lord, please help me treat my family with the respect and kindness they deserve. Help me to have patience with my siblings and point them toward You.

PEACEFUL ATTITUDE

Do all that you can to live in peace with everyone.
ROMANS 12:18 NLT

You have days when you might not feel like living at peace with everyone. Maybe you didn't sleep well and you wake up grumpy. Or maybe you had a bad dream that you can't stop thinking about, and it's bothering you. Or maybe you have no idea why you are annoyed—you just are—and you want people to leave you alone for a while!

The best thing to do when you feel like that is to find a quiet place just to be with God. You might even need to ask your friends and family to give you a little space while you go talk to God about the way you're feeling. Even if you don't understand why you feel the way you do, God does! So take your problems to Him first, and allow Him to help you sort them out. Ask Him to change your attitude as He works on your heart. Then you can enjoy peaceful relationships with others because you know that the God who created you is working on your problems with you.

Father, sometimes I can get pretty grumpy with other people. I'm sorry about that. Please help me take my thoughts and feelings to You first. Change my attitude to be more like Yours.

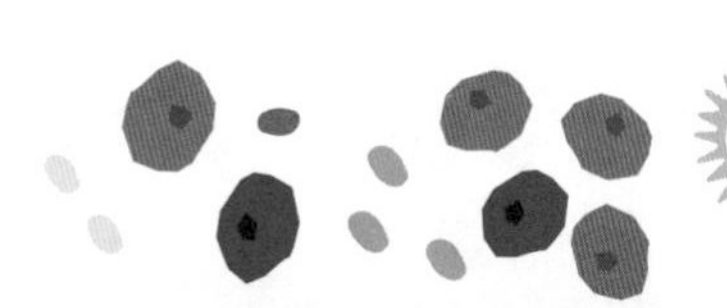

CONFLICT AND PATIENCE

A hot-tempered person stirs up conflict,
but the one who is patient calms a quarrel.
PROVERBS 15:18 NIV

Do you know anyone who just loves to argue? The ability to argue a point to defend one's beliefs is something that can be used for good. But some people argue just to be right, and it seems like they really don't care much about other people's feelings. These people have a lot to say, and they rarely ever listen. This is the kind of person who stirs up trouble.

A patient person, on the other hand, cares more about others and is good at listening. This is the kind of person you want for a friend. If you know someone at school or have someone in your family who stirs up trouble, pray for that person. Ask God to step in and soften their heart. Sometimes they don't even know how much they hurt others. Ask God to show them. And work on being a patient person who lights up other people's lives.

Father, please forgive me for the times when I've picked a fight with someone else without really listening. Help me to be a patient person who cares for others. Help me to light up the lives of people around me. I want to point them to You.

TRUE LOVE

Love is patient, love is kind. It does not envy, it does not boast, it is not proud.
1 CORINTHIANS 13:4 NIV

You'll meet a lot of people in this world who have no idea what true love is. True love is nothing like what you see in the movies or on social media (#truelove). Our enemy has confused the world into thinking that love equals affection, nice feelings, and attraction, but that simply isn't true. Love is a choice. True love has very little to do with your feelings.

Hear this truth: You can actually love someone without liking them very much! Wait. . .what?! Yep, it's true. That's true, biblical love. For example, when someone you know gossips about you or your sister takes your favorite shirt without asking and stains it, you can respond without hurting them back. That is a loving action—even if you don't feel like you like that person very much in the moment.

Married couples who've been married for decades choose to love and serve one another even if they don't "feel" like loving and serving. That's true love. That's the kind of love that lasts.

Dear God, please help me to understand what true love is. Help me choose to love people no matter how I might feel about them. Thank You that You love me no matter what.

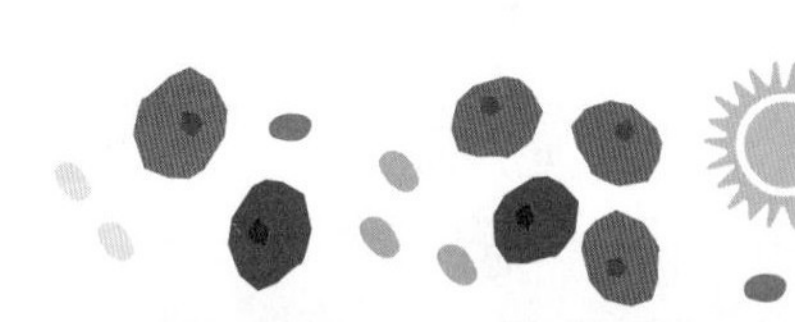

PATIENCE FOR OTHERS

Always be humble and gentle. Be patient with each other, making allowance for each other's faults because of your love.

Ephesians 4:2 NLT

You can probably think of at least a couple of people who really annoy you. Maybe they always have a bad attitude or are extremely sarcastic. Have you ever thought about why they act the way they do? Maybe they aren't getting their needs met from their parents or they're being bullied and are trying to get attention and affection from anyone else they can. There is always a reason why people act the way they do, even if they don't know it themselves.

But God knows! That's why you should pray for the people who bother you. God knows exactly why they act the way they do, and *your* prayers can help change that person's heart—and yours in the process! Nobody is perfect, and even your best friend will act in ways that bother you at some time or another. Make allowance for that because of God's love living inside you. Be patient and gentle with others. Start this morning by praying for the people you know you'll probably see today. Pray blessings and love over them.

Father, I don't understand why people act the way they do, but I pray You would help me show love and kindness to them anyways.

RELATIONSHIPS

Do not envy the wicked, do not desire their company; for their hearts plot violence, and their lips talk about making trouble. By wisdom a house is built, and through understanding it is established; through knowledge its rooms are filled with rare and beautiful treasures.

PROVERBS 24:1–4 NIV

This proverb begins by explaining the trouble we can get into when we are in relationships that don't honor God—with people who don't honor God. But the Bible says that by wisdom a house is built, a home is built, relationships are built.

If taken literally, a wise person can have the knowledge and understanding to build a house with their own hands and fill it with beautiful treasures. But this proverb has a deeper meaning: we build our homes and families with wisdom and understanding that come from God. Our "treasures" are people and family values such as love and respect.

When we honor God in our relationships, His will comes first. We seek to please Him as we relate to one another. Ask God to be the center of all your relationships so that they will be honoring to Him.

Lord, I pray for wisdom as I build relationships in my life. Help me listen to Your Spirit as You lead me toward or away from people. Be at the center of all I do, Lord.

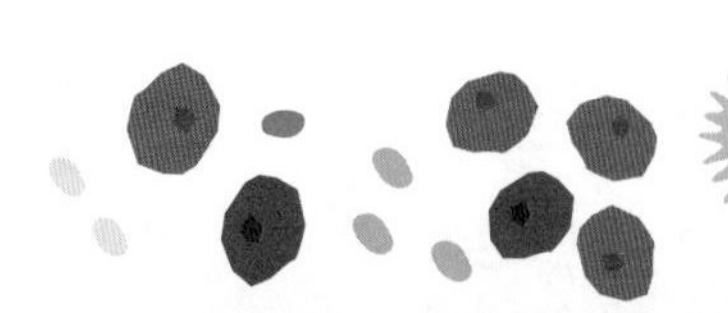

TRUST

Trust God from the bottom of your heart; don't try to figure out everything on your own. Listen for God's voice in everything you do, everywhere you go; he's the one who will keep you on track. Don't assume that you know it all. Run to God! Run from evil!

Proverbs 3:5 msg

Good morning! It's a new day and a new topic: trust! Today's verse is really good advice. Read through it again, slowly. The key points?

- Trust God.
- Don't try to figure out everything on your own.
- Listen for God's voice in everything you do.
- God will keep you on track.
- You don't know it all.
- Run from evil and toward God.

Those are some good words to live by. Highlight them. Write them down. Tape them to your mirror. If you were writing a book on trust, those might even be the chapter titles you could use! As we dive into what it means to trust God, pray for God to open your heart more and draw you closer.

Lord, help me learn to trust You from the bottom of my heart. Give me the desire and urgency to run from evil and toward You. I want to listen for Your voice in everything I do and everywhere I go.

TRUST GOD

The LORD will work out his plans for my life—for your faithful love, O LORD, endures forever. Don't abandon me, for you made me.
PSALM 138:8 NLT

God's love for you is unfailing and faithful. He is with you always. He is listening, and He knows everything about you. You are His princess, and He will never abandon you. You are a daughter of the King of all kings, and He has wonderful plans for your life. All these truths you can find in scripture! Even the painful things that happen in life, God will miraculously turn into good things if you trust in Him!

Really? One hundred percent! Take a look: Romans 8:28 (NIV) says, "We know that in all things God works for the good of those who love him, who have been called according to his purpose." God is working everything out for your good. That's a promise. And you can trust that God always keeps His promises. He's the only one you can always trust no matter what. Even the most loving and well-meaning parent messes up sometimes. God never does. You can trust Him with your life.

Lord, You never mess up, and You love me perfectly. That's so amazing! I trust You with my life.

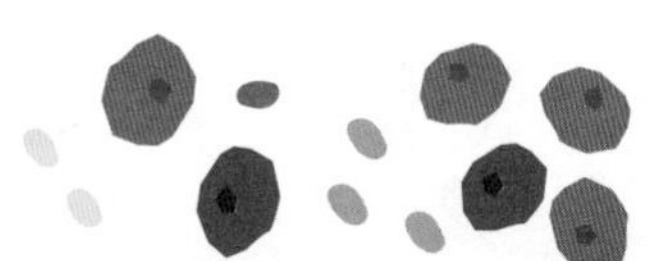

STRONG ROOTS

"Blessed are those who trust in the LORD and have made the LORD their hope and confidence. They are like trees planted along a riverbank, with roots that reach deep into the water. Such trees are not bothered by the heat or worried by long months of drought. Their leaves stay green, and they never stop producing fruit."

JEREMIAH 17:7–8 NLT

Our family loves canoeing. I'm always impressed by the humongous trees that live along the river. You can see their giant root systems as they wind their way into the water. The trees are healthy and huge. Even if the river looks a little dry, the trees continue to thrive because their roots go deep.

The Bible tells us that when we trust in God and put our hope and confidence in Him, we'll be blessed—kind of like a tree along the river with deep roots. A tree with deep roots won't get toppled when storms come. It's strongly attached to the ground. It grows deep and is able to find the water it needs to stay hydrated during a dry spell.

Lord, I want Your blessing and favor on my life. I pray that You would grow my faith deep into the roots of Your love. I want to build my life upon You and Your truth.

TRUST IN HARD TIMES

We continue to shout our praise even when we're hemmed in with troubles, because we know how troubles can develop passionate patience in us.
ROMANS 5:3 MSG

When you're going through some hard times, it's easy to get discouraged. You want things to change, and you want them to change quickly! Sometimes it can be really hard to keep a good attitude when you need things to change so badly.

But hard times can turn good if we allow God to work in them. We learn to trust God more in times of trouble. We cry out to God a lot more during hard times. We seek Him because we know deep down that He's the only one who can actually change things.

Hard times teach us to be patient too. Hard things give us an opportunity to trust God's word. Psalm 32:7–8 (NIV) says, "You are my hiding place; you will protect me from trouble and surround me with songs of deliverance. I will instruct you and teach you in the way you should go; I will counsel you with my loving eye on you."

Father, I give You praise even during hard times. I trust Your Word, and I choose to wait patiently and watch with great expectation while You turn bad things into good life lessons.

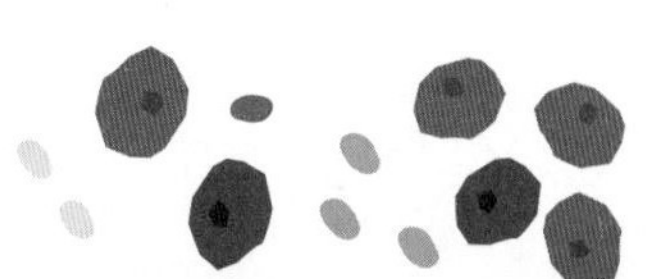

MORNING MANNA

Each morning everyone gathered as much as they needed, and when the sun grew hot, it melted away.
EXODUS 16:21 NIV

Have you heard about manna? Manna was the miracle food God sent down from heaven for the Israelites when they were wandering in the desert for forty years. They ran out of food, so God sent a flaky substance that the Bible says tasted like honey wafers (Exodus 16).

The Israelites had to go and collect it every morning, and they couldn't store it or it would spoil. The people tried to hoard extra manna (because, you know, people!), but the hoarded collection became full of maggots. Miraculously, they were given instructions to collect a double portion one day a week before the Sabbath, but their Sabbath collection never spoiled.

God saw their need and took care of them daily. The Israelites had to learn to trust that God would come through and meet their needs every morning.

God wants us to depend on Him like that too. Are you coming to Him every morning, trusting that He'll meet your daily needs?

Lord, You've taught us to pray, "Give us this day, our daily bread." I'm thankful for how You meet my daily needs—not just for food but for strength and courage and all the things I need for this day.

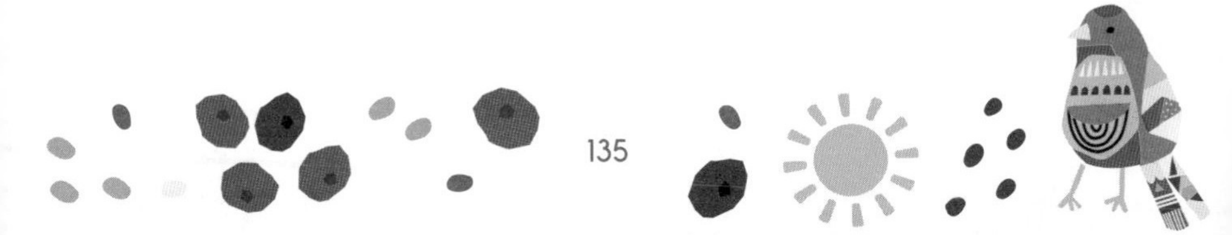

TRUST GOD'S PROMISE

Be joyful in hope, patient in affliction, faithful in prayer.
ROMANS 12:12 NIV

Just like the Israelites receiving their daily manna, you can trust that God sees you and knows exactly what you need when you need it. Isn't that amazing? The God of creation sees *you* and knows exactly what you need right at this very moment. Let that sink in for a minute.

Need to see that in black and white? Here you go: Philippians 4:19 (NIV) says, "My God will meet all your needs according to the riches of his glory in Christ Jesus." That's a promise! So we can be patient when things seem tough because we trust God's promise.

And while we wait, God wants us to be faithful in prayer. Talk to God about all of your needs and thoughts. Repent when you need to and ask for help to change. Ask God to care for those around you too. When you say you're going to pray for someone, write it down and do it. Prayer changes things! James 5:16 (NIV) says, "The prayer of a righteous person is powerful and effective."

Okay, today's devotion has three great scriptures in it to write down and remember! Got your pen?

Father, thank You for hearing my prayers and for meeting all of my needs. I trust in Your promises!

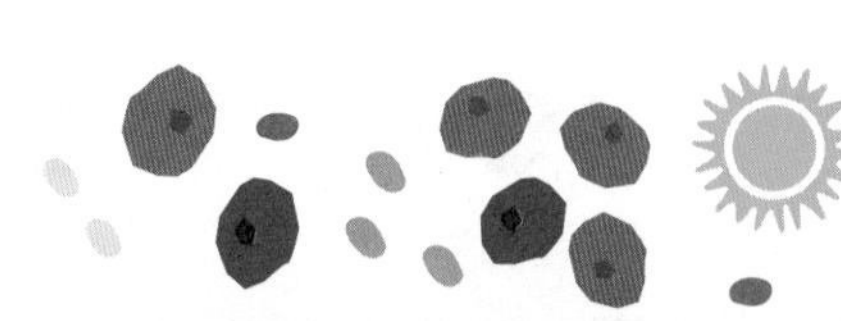

GIFTS FROM GOD

God has us where he wants us, with all the time in this world and the next to shower grace and kindness upon us in Christ Jesus. Saving is all his idea, and all his work. All we do is trust him enough to let him do it. It's God's gift from start to finish!

EPHESIANS 2:7–8 MSG

Do you see God as someone who showers grace and kindness upon you each day? That's exactly what He wants to do. He loves you so much that He sent His Son to take away all the sin from your heart and make you righteous in His sight. All you have to do is trust Him!

Think of a mother who delights in getting her children special presents for birthdays and Christmas. She searches and plans to find exactly the perfect gift to make her child smile. The Bible tells us that even sinful people know how to give good gifts to their children, so "how much more will your heavenly Father give good gifts to those who ask him" (Matthew 7:11 NLT).

God is a good and loving Father who wants to shower you with His love. He is full of good gifts for you as you stay close to Him.

Lord, thank You for blessing me over and over again.

TIME TO REPENT

If we [freely] admit that we have sinned and confess our sins, He is faithful and just [true to His own nature and promises], and will forgive our sins and cleanse us continually from all unrighteousness [our wrongdoing, everything not in conformity with His will and purpose].

1 John 1:9 AMP

None of us is perfect, and we all make mistakes from time to time. Some of us forget God for a while until we realize how much we've messed up without Him.

When you've messed up, turn back to God and start to trust Him again—really trust Him. This is called repentance. When you repent, you turn away from sin and turn toward God.

He already knows what you've done, but He wants to talk with you about it. He wants to help you through it and give you peace. He doesn't want you to carry shame with you. Shame weighs you down and prevents you from being effective in God's kingdom.

When you trust God with everything you have, He gives you the ability to do good and to be faithful. His resurrection power is alive and at work within you.

Father, I know I've messed up. Will You please forgive me and change my heart? Remove my shame and show me a better way. Help me to trust You more.

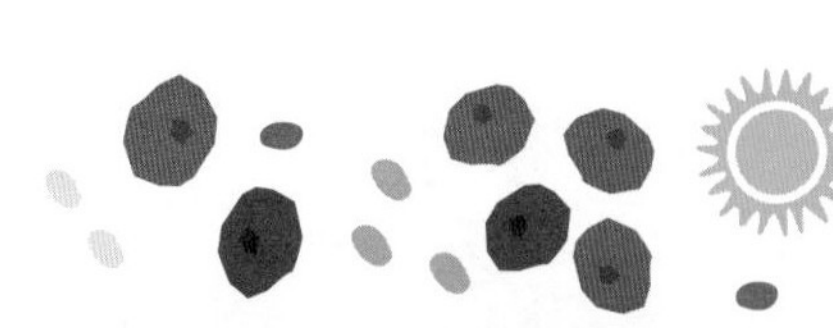

MUSTARD SEED FAITH

"I tell you the truth, if you had faith even as small as a mustard seed, you could say to this mountain, 'Move from here to there,' and it would move. Nothing would be impossible."
MATTHEW 17:20 NLT

Jesus' disciples couldn't heal a boy who was having seizures, so they went to Jesus and asked Him why. The disciples may have been trying to handle the situation in their own power instead of depending on God. So He told them about the mustard seed.

Have you ever seen a mustard seed? Look for a jar of them the next time you're at the grocery store. They are very tiny! Jesus tells us that even if we have faith that small, He will show up in *big* ways! It's not the size of our faith that counts; it's the power of God that makes the difference. God doesn't want us to trust in ourselves and in our own abilities. Faith is all about putting our trust in the living God and knowing that when we are weak, He is strong!

When you are facing mountains in your life, think about the mustard seed. Ask God to remind you that He is much bigger than your mountain!

Lord, sometimes I feel like my faith is too small. Remind me that You're bigger than everything I'll ever face.

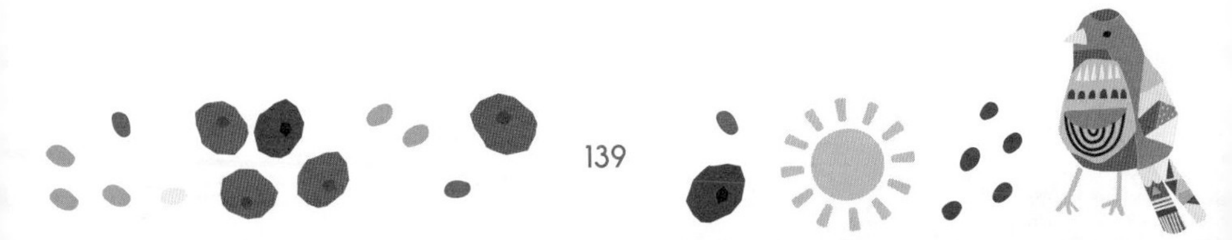

SAFE IN GOD'S HANDS

I trust in you, Lord; I say, "You are my God." My times are in your hands; deliver me from the hands of my enemies, from those who pursue me.
Psalm 31:14–15 NIV

Trusting God daily keeps you from being sucked into the constant craziness of life. When you feel overwhelmed with the world's craziness, first of all get off your phone and spend some time with God without a million distractions.

Time alone with God makes our problems seem so much smaller when we think about heaven and all that God has planned for those who love Him. While life may be hard and confusing at times, we know that all of our times are in God's hands. He sees everything we're going through and has a miraculous plan to make things right.

So when trouble comes knocking at your door (or a notification shows up on your phone), you don't have to freak out! You can say, "I trust in You, Lord! My times are in Your hands. I know You've got this. I trust Your faithfulness. This looks hard, but I know it'll be okay."

You are safe in God's hands.

Father, please give me the desire to seek You without distraction! I need that precious time with You to keep my head on straight. Thanks for keeping me safe in Your hands.

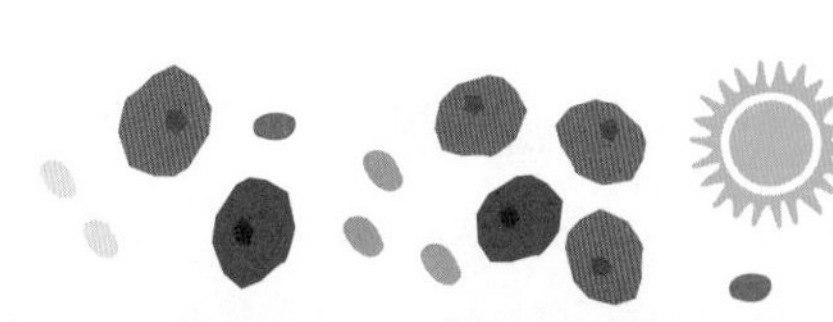

YOUR REFUGE

How great is Your goodness, which You have stored up for those who [reverently] fear You, which You have prepared for those who take refuge in You, before the sons of man!
PSALM 31:19 AMP

The Bible talks a lot about God being our refuge. Take a look:

- "God is our refuge and strength, an ever-present help in trouble." (Psalm 46:1 NIV)
- "Trust in him at all times, you people; pour out your hearts to him, for God is our refuge." (Psalm 62:8 NIV)
- "Show me the wonders of your great love, you who save by your right hand those who take refuge in you from their foes." (Psalm 17:7 NIV)

And that's only a few of the verses about God being our refuge. So, what is a refuge? The biblical definition is a place of safety or shelter. It's also a place for you to escape danger.

When you trust God, He becomes your refuge. He will shelter you Himself. Just like when you run to your room and hop on your bed to be alone, get comfortable, and even escape, God wants to be that safe and comfortable hiding place for you.

Lord, I like this idea of You being my refuge and safe place. Teach me to come to You for shelter, safety, and comfort. Thanks for always being there for me!

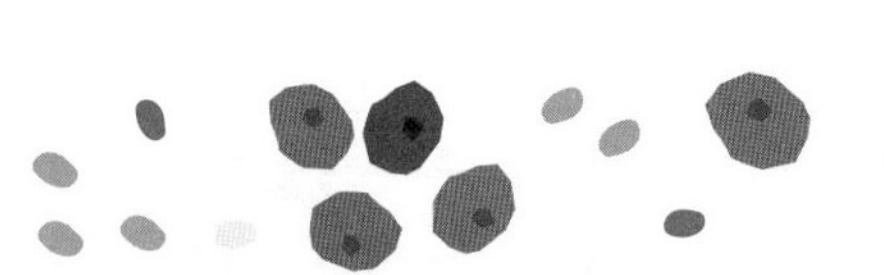

YOUR WALK WITH GOD

You have rescued me from death; you have kept my feet from slipping. So now I can walk in your presence, O God, in your life-giving light.
Psalm 56:13 NLT

What does your walk with God look like? The Christian life is not just reading a Bible verse each morning and checking God off your list for the day. It is not being a regular member at church and leaving faith in the box until the next Sunday.

Walking with God is just what it sounds like. Can you picture yourself hand in hand with Jesus as you venture through this world? It's a moment-by-moment thing. First Thessalonians 5:16–18 (NIV) says, "Rejoice always, pray continually, give thanks in all circumstances; for this is God's will for you in Christ Jesus."

The Christian life is a never-ending walk and talk with Jesus. It is knowing Him, loving Him, trusting Him, and worshipping Him in each moment. It's inviting God into every conversation you have, every thought you think, and everything you do. The Bible promises that we can walk in God's presence each and every moment!

Father, help me to be constantly aware of Your presence in my life. I want to know You more. I'm taking hold of Your hand as we walk together. I want to share all my moments with You.

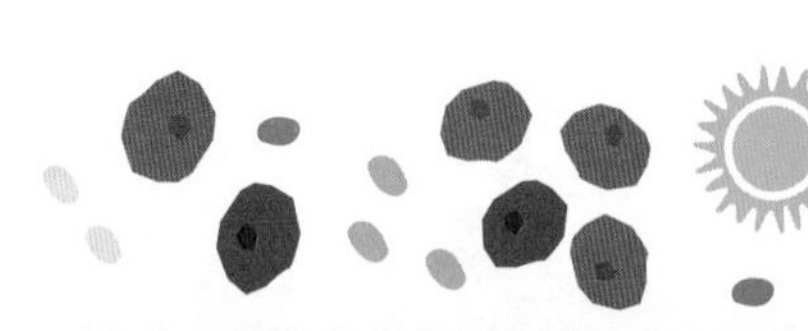

HAND IN HAND

Those who know your name trust in you, for you, Lord, have never forsaken those who seek you.
Psalm 9:10 NIV

Imagine yourself holding Jesus' hand on a journey through the wilderness. You come across something that makes your heart beat faster. You're scared. There's a wild beast coming right at you. Does Jesus still have hold of your hand? What happens? Take this journey further and imagine other scenarios. What does Jesus want you to know?

When you walk with God, you experience His absolute faithfulness. He has promised never to leave you or forsake you (Hebrews 13:5). This brings trust—a deep knowing—that God is ultimately good and has your best interests in mind.

Things still happen along the way that don't make any sense to us at the time. We experience pain and sadness that come with living in a messed-up world. But as we seek Jesus and keep a tight hold on His hand, we begin to see purpose in our troubles. He turns everything around for our good and His glory! He has purpose in everything. He is just, He is righteous, and He is good.

Jesus, I trust that You will never let me go. I know I can come to You and find shelter and safety with my hand in Yours.

HOLDING IT TOGETHER

We look at this Son and see the God who cannot be seen. We look at this Son and see God's original purpose in everything created. For everything, absolutely everything, above and below, visible and invisible, rank after rank after rank of angels—everything got started in him and finds its purpose in him. He was there before any of it came into existence and holds it all together right up to this moment.

COLOSSIANS 1:15–17 MSG

God is over all and in all and through all. He holds all things together—"right up to this moment." He knows everything and is certainly aware of everything that concerns you. Pinch yourself. Yep, you heard me. Touch your skin. Is your body still functioning as God designed it? A mass of cells with organs that are miraculously working together to keep you alive? Then God is still alive, at work, and holding all things together—including your very own body!

Is there a problem or an issue that you are holding on to and trying to figure out all by yourself? Bring it to Jesus. If something in your life feels too big or too small for God, remember that He holds *everything* together. He cares about what You care about. Trust Him to help.

Lord, thanks for the reminder that You're holding everything together—including me!

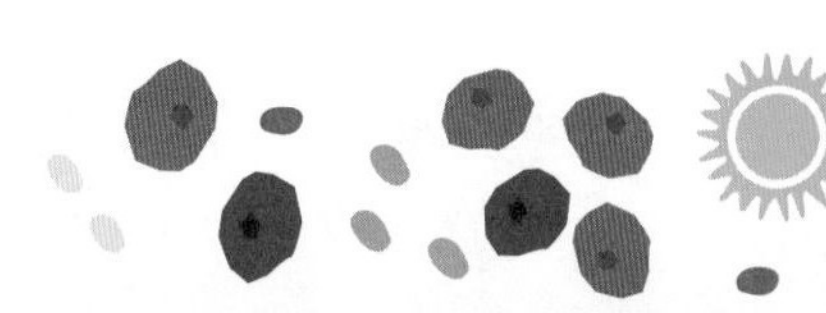

STRAIGHT FROM GOD

So trust him absolutely, people; lay your lives on the line for him. God is a safe place to be. . . . God said this once and for all; how many times have I heard it repeated? "Strength comes straight from God."

Psalm 62:8, 11 MSG

Have you been working hard at something lately? Maybe school or sports? Are you trying to make yourself stronger in those areas? The important thing to remember is that strength comes from God Himself. He can help! Bring to mind everything you are currently working hard on. God has all the answers and is very interested in helping you! Maybe it's algebra, maybe it's gymnastics, maybe it's basketball or trigonometry. He can help you think clearly and get stronger.

As His Word promises, God is a safe place to be, and you can trust Him absolutely. Both when you mess up and when you succeed, God is safe. He delights in you. He shares your sorrows and your joys. Allow Him to be with you in those times. Bring your successes and failures to Jesus now, and let Him love you in them.

Lord God, You have the answers I'm looking for. You are the source of strength that I'm needing. I bring You my successes and my failures. I don't have to perform for You. You love me no matter what.

THE LIST

Delight yourself in the Lord, and He will give you the desires and petitions of your heart.
Psalm 37:4 AMP

Let's start a little project this morning. This might take you a few days or a week. That's okay!

Put a date at the top of a fresh journal page or clean piece of paper, and start writing out your needs. Then move on to the things you really want, like a birthday or Christmas list. Now write what you think you might want to do with your life and the things you might need to get you there (college money, a car, career goals, etc.).

When you've finished your list, hold it before God and ask Him to lead you. Thank Him for the needs that He has already provided. Talk to Him about your wants. Do they align with God's will for you? Are they good and God honoring? Do you feel like you don't have enough patience to wait for the things you need and want? Ask God to give you wisdom and patience. Trust Him with your list.

Father, I give You all my wants and needs. Help me to delight myself in You alone, not in the things I think I might want. I know You will bless me in the way that You think is best.

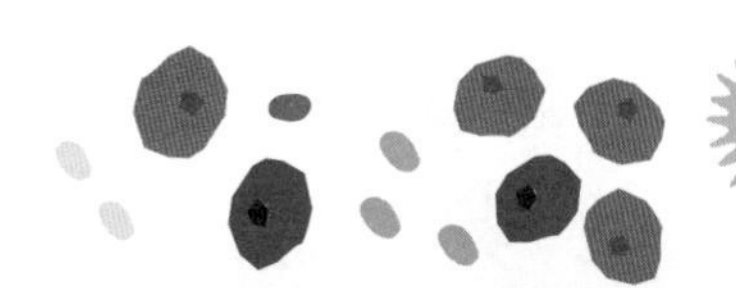

OUR SHEPHERD

"I am the good shepherd. The good shepherd lays down his life for the sheep."
JOHN 10:11 NIV

To love and trust Jesus, you have to know and understand certain things about Him. Jesus said in John 10:27–30 (NIV), "My sheep listen to my voice; I know them, and they follow me. I give them eternal life, and they shall never perish; no one will snatch them out of my hand. My Father, who has given them to me, is greater than all; no one can snatch them out of my Father's hand. I and the Father are one."

We don't see shepherds too much these days, but back in Bible times, shepherds were common. A good and gentle shepherd would love and care for his sheep with compassion and kindness. When the shepherd walked ahead of them, they followed him because they knew his voice. Jesus calls us His sheep, and He lovingly cares for each of us!

Today's verse reminds us that our Shepherd even gave His very life for us! When we get to know His voice, we can be sure we're following someone we can trust. As you start your day, be listening for His voice in each moment. He is there, leading and guiding you!

Jesus, I trust You and I know that I can count on You to lead me to the right places.

YOU CAN TRUST HIM

He didn't tiptoe around God's promise asking cautiously skeptical questions. He plunged into the promise and came up strong, ready for God, sure that God would make good on what he had said. That's why it is said, "Abraham was declared fit before God by trusting God to set him right." But it's not just Abraham; it's also us! The same thing gets said about us when we embrace and believe the One who brought Jesus to life when the conditions were equally hopeless. The sacrificed Jesus made us fit for God, set us right with God.

ROMANS 4:20–25 MSG

In the Old Testament, God promised Abraham that he would become the father of many nations. Abraham trusted that God would fulfill that promise, even when it seemed hopeless. Abraham was really old when his first child was born. But God kept His promise. And Jesus Himself, the Savior of the world, came from Abraham's family line.

Are you or a close friend or family member facing a situation that seems a bit hopeless? You can trust God to keep His promises. Are you facing a mountain of problems? Bring your anxiety and fears to Jesus and ask Him to remind you of His faithfulness.

Father, just like Abraham, I want to trust You wholeheartedly! Please remove all my doubts and fears.

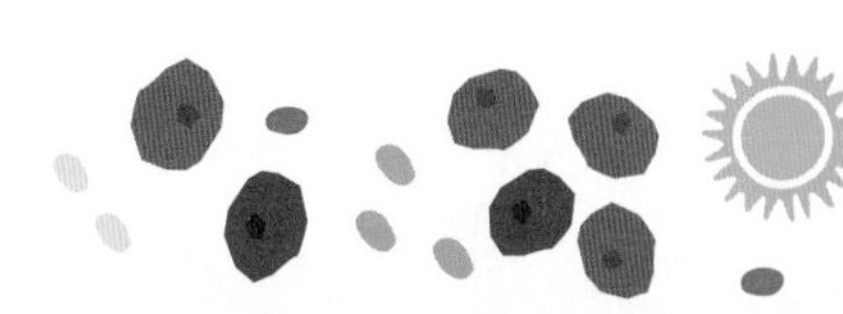

UNLIMITED POWER

God made the earth by His power; He established the world by His wisdom and by His understanding and skill He has stretched out the heavens. When He utters His voice, there is a tumult of waters in the heavens, and He causes the clouds and the mist to ascend from the end of the earth; He makes lightning for the rain, and brings out the wind from His treasuries and from His storehouses.

JEREMIAH 10:12–13 AMP

Close your eyes and imagine this scripture happening. Imagine God creating the world, stretching out the heavens, and speaking the waters into existence with His voice. The same God who stretched out the heavens and causes the wind to blow is the God who loves and cares about you. How amazing is that?

When you think about God's unlimited power and His love for you, what happens to your problems? Do you trust that God can handle anything you have going on? Take some time to bring your cares and worries to God in prayer. As He lifts those burdens off your shoulders, thank Him for His faithfulness to you today!

I'm amazed at Your power, Lord God. I bring You everything on my heart this morning. I know You're powerful enough to take care of everything that weighs me down.

CLEAN CONVICTION

Don't you see how wonderfully kind, tolerant, and patient God is with you? Does this mean nothing to you? Can't you see that his kindness is intended to turn you from your sin?

ROMANS 2:4 NLT

Some people live in fear that they're always doing something wrong or that God is always mad at them. But here's the thing: you can trust God's loving Spirit inside you to convict you when you're doing something that needs correcting.

Conviction happens when God pricks our hearts about something that does not line up with His will. The amazing thing is that God's conviction is clean. He doesn't want you wallowing in shame and self-pity. Today's verse tells us that it's God's loving-kindness that brings us to repentance. His love is what draws out the darkness and brings it to light, turning us away from sin and toward Him.

Ask God to shine His light on any sin in your life. Repent of that sin and turn back toward God. Then move forward in His loving-kindness and grace!

Lord, I'm glad I have Your Spirit at work in my heart to lovingly show me where I need to change. Shine Your light on anything I need to make right. Thank You for Your grace and love.

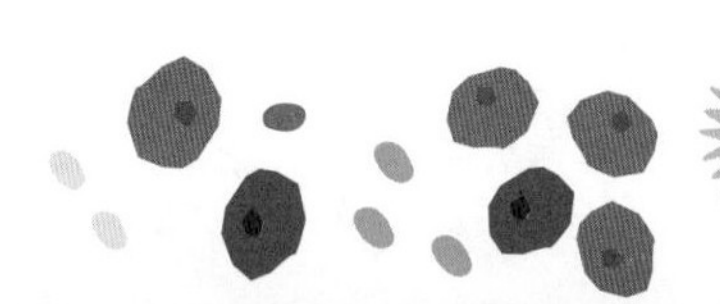

JESUS CALMS THE STORM

He got up and rebuked the winds and the waves, and it was completely calm. The men were amazed and asked, "What kind of man is this? Even the winds and the waves obey him!"
MATTHEW 8:26–27 NIV

Storms can be pretty scary, right? Wind and lightning can do great damage. Loud thunder and flashes of lightning are enough to stress the bravest adult. Now imagine that happening while you're on a boat in the middle of a large body of water.

That very thing happened to Jesus and His disciples. But Jesus was asleep when the storm started. And even though the disciples were experienced fishermen who knew their way around boats and storms, this storm had them worried. The waves were sweeping over the boat, and the disciples thought they were going to drown! They woke Jesus, begging for His help.

The good thing is that they went to the right person for help! Jesus spoke to the wind and waves and told them to stop. And they did! Jesus still holds that same power over all of nature today. You can always ask Him for help.

Lord, I'm amazed at the power You have, that all of nature responds to Your commands. Please give me the faith to believe in Your power.

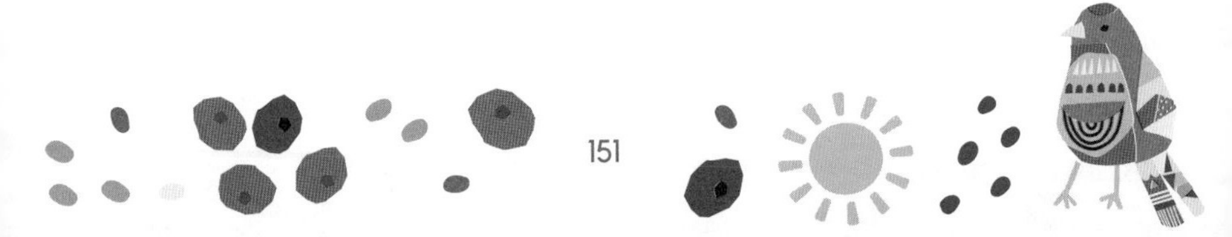

VERY PRESENT HELP

You, God, see the trouble of the afflicted; you consider their grief and take it in hand. The victims commit themselves to you; you are the helper of the fatherless.
PSALM 10:14 NIV

The Bible tells us that God helps us in times of trouble. In fact, Psalm 46:1 (NIV) says that God is "an ever-present help in trouble." Think about that for a minute: God is *always present*—He is with you this very moment as you read these words. His power and comfort are constantly available to you. He is good, and He wants to show His goodness to you on a daily basis. Right now!

When you focus on bad things and worry about stuff that hasn't even happened yet, you forget about God. It's almost like you're imagining a future without Him! Be honest: when you worry about something in the future, is Jesus in that picture in your mind?

When you focus on God and talk to Him instead of worrying, He actually shows Himself to you in each moment. We may live in a broken world, but we have great hope because God is with us and His perfect plan is trustworthy!

Father, thank You for being with me in each moment. Forgive me for the times when I worry. Please replace my worries with Your peace.

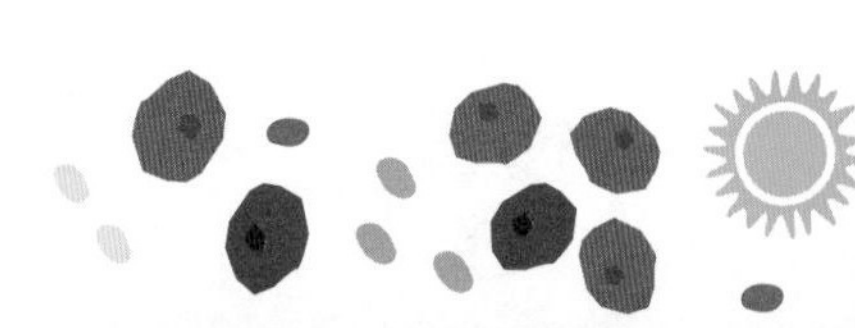

THE HAND OF JESUS

While he was saying this, a synagogue leader came and knelt before him and said, "My daughter has just died. But come and put your hand on her, and she will live."

MATTHEW 9:18 NIV

Jesus was talking to some people when a desperate man came and asked Jesus for help. His young daughter had just died. A crowd was mourning her death outside the man's home, and they did not believe that Jesus could bring the dead to life. They even laughed at Jesus when He arrived at the house. But the girl's father believed.

Jesus took the girl by her hand, and she got up! To the crowd, this situation seemed hopeless. The girl was dead. What could anyone do? But the father trusted that Jesus was who He said He was. He went to Jesus and asked for help, and Jesus answered. Ask Jesus to take your hand like He took this little girl's hand. Jesus loves you, and you are very important to Him! Your faith in the God of miracles will make all the difference in your life. Jesus is with you. He takes hold of your hand.

Jesus, please take hold of my hand and walk with me every day of my life on this earth. I'm thankful for Your love. I trust You to do the impossible.

THE VOICES YOU HEAR

God did not send his Son into the world to condemn the world, but to save the world through him.

JOHN 3:17 NIV

I saw a picture of someone's journal page on social media that listed the characteristics of God's voice versus the characteristics of our enemy. It noted that God's voice stills, leads, reassures, enlightens, comforts, calms, and convicts while our enemy's voice rushes, pushes, frightens, confuses, discourages, worries, obsesses, and condemns you. Which voice are you listening to?

People can take on the characteristics of our enemy, so it's important to choose your friends wisely. Many times people aren't aware that they do this, so please beware of others (even well-meaning friends or family members) who say things that frighten, confuse, and condemn you. That is not loving, and it is not from God. Remember what we've learned already: when God convicts you of sin, He does so with kindness that leads you back to Him. He never shames or condemns you.

You get to choose which voices you listen to. Don't give airtime to the enemy. When condemning and frightening voices come up in your mind, send them away in Jesus' name!

Father, please help me to be wise in the relationships I form and the people I allow to speak into my life. Thank You for Your loving voice that calls me back to the protection of Your arms.

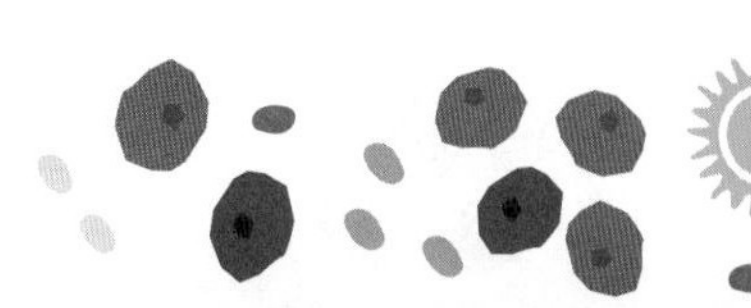

ROOTS

I pray that from his glorious, unlimited resources he will empower you with inner strength through his Spirit. Then Christ will make his home in your hearts as you trust in him. Your roots will grow down into God's love and keep you strong.

EPHESIANS 3:16–17 NLT

Having strong roots is important to God. Take a look at Colossians 2:7 (NLT): "Let your roots grow down into him, and let your lives be built on him. Then your faith will grow strong in the truth you were taught, and you will overflow with thankfulness."

When we think of roots, our first thought is often of tree roots. Then we might think of family roots and being tied to a certain location because our family is there. Today's verse is a beautiful promise for Christ's followers: as you learn to trust Him, Christ makes His home in your heart. And then your roots grow down into God's love, keeping you strong.

If you were to draw a picture of this happening, what would it look like? Picture your roots growing deep into God's love.

Jesus, thank You for making Your home in my heart! Strengthen my roots and let them grow deep into Your love. I want Your favor and blessing in my life. Help me to trust You with all my heart.

JESUS IN EVERYTHING

I will teach you wisdom's ways and lead you in straight paths.
PROVERBS 4:11 NLT

Have you ever heard of deism? It's a belief that God created the world and left people to manage it. Deists believe that God doesn't interact with humans. But that's not at all what the Bible teaches.

First Corinthians 1:9 (AMP) says, "God is faithful [He is reliable, trustworthy and ever true to His promise—He can be depended on], and through Him you were called into fellowship with His Son, Jesus Christ our Lord."

You were called into fellowship with Jesus. That means Jesus wants a relationship with you, a deep and growing friendship. He cares about your plans and wants to be involved in them. He is there to help you make decisions and will guide you as you learn to listen to His voice.

When we forget that God wants to help us make choices, we get confused and anxious. When we leave Jesus out of the decision-making process, we unnecessarily encounter lots of problems.

Jesus, I trust that You care about everything I have on my schedule. I invite You to be a part of every plan and every decision. Remind me that You're here when I start to forget You. Help me to be willing to change course if I feel You leading me in a different way. Give me ears to hear.

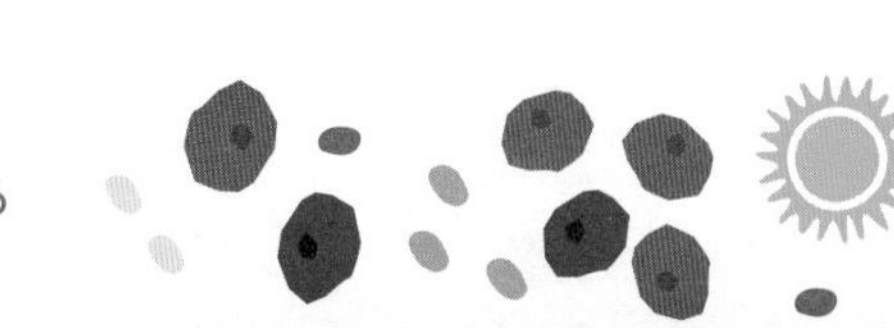

NO MORE WORRIES

"If God cares so wonderfully for wildflowers that are here today and thrown into the fire tomorrow, he will certainly care for you. Why do you have so little faith?"
MATTHEW 6:30 NLT

Our enemy loves to distract us and get us to worry. Worry is picturing the future without Jesus in it! When we worry, our focus is never on Christ—so the enemy wins! Stress and worry are signs that we aren't trusting God very much. So what can be done about that? Go to God and repent. Turn away from worry and turn toward God.

When people and things are big in your life, God doesn't have the room He needs to be big in your world. And that means you have idols in your heart. Anything that comes between you and God is an idol. Maybe it's someone you love, and their opinion of you matters more than God. Or maybe your desire for something is so great that it is getting in the way of what God wants to do in your life. Lay all of these at the feet of Jesus and allow Him to make changes. With idols removed from your heart, God gets bigger and worries get smaller.

Father, please highlight and remove any idols in my heart. I trust that You will care for me. Please increase my faith!

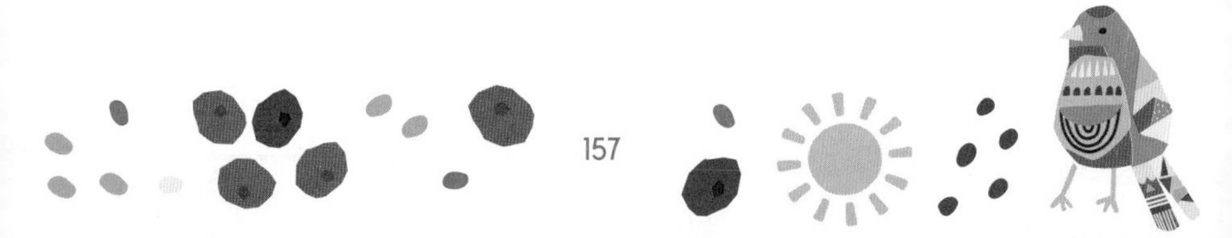

STAY ON YOUR OWN PATH

Now you've got my feet on the life path, all radiant from the shining of your face. Ever since you took my hand, I'm on the right way.

PSALM 16:11 MSG

Have you ever tried to fix a problem that wasn't yours to fix? Maybe you tried to help a friend with a difficult relationship. Or maybe you got involved in a situation that wasn't even your problem and ended up making it worse. Those can be tough life lessons to learn.

Not every problem is yours to fix. Not every ministry is yours to get involved in. Not every path is yours to take. God wants you to acknowledge and come to Him before and during your plans.

Does this mean that if you've made a bad choice and taken a wrong path you're on your own? Absolutely not. God has promised never to leave you! Trust Him to help you get back on the path that was meant for you. Yeah, it might be a little messy trying to get out of a situation you've put yourself in! But God is faithful even when we make a mess of things.

Father, please help me to get back on the right path. I want to trust You with all my heart and come to You first before I decide to get involved in any situation.

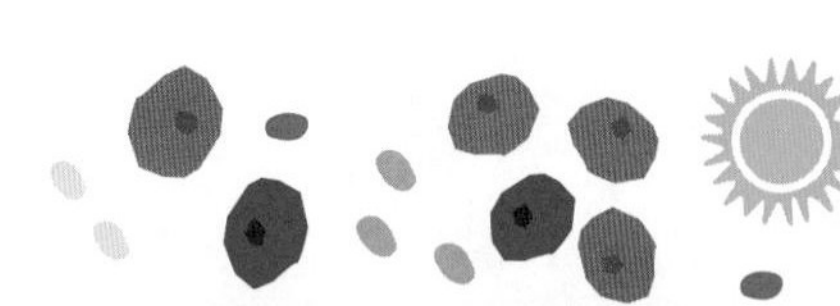

BE TRUSTWORTHY

"Just say a simple, 'Yes, I will,' or 'No, I won't.' Anything beyond this is from the evil one."
MATTHEW 5:37 NLT

Has someone ever told you a lie? It hurts, doesn't it? It makes you not want to trust that person ever again. And honestly, it's hard to trust that person again, right?

Jesus was teaching a large crowd of people, and it was really important for them to know that He wants His followers to be trustworthy. When you say you're going to do something, do it. Instead of always saying "I promise" to do something, simply show that you will carry through by doing it.

When you tell your sister you're going to return her sweater as soon as you get home from school, do what you said you would. Otherwise, she might not let you borrow it next time.

Your parents want to trust you too. If you say you're going to be home at a certain time, make sure you are! And if something comes up preventing that, call and discuss the problem with them as soon as possible. The more trustworthy you are, the more privileges and responsibilities you'll be given. This will prove true your whole life.

Jesus, I want people to trust me. Help me to do what I say I'm going to do.

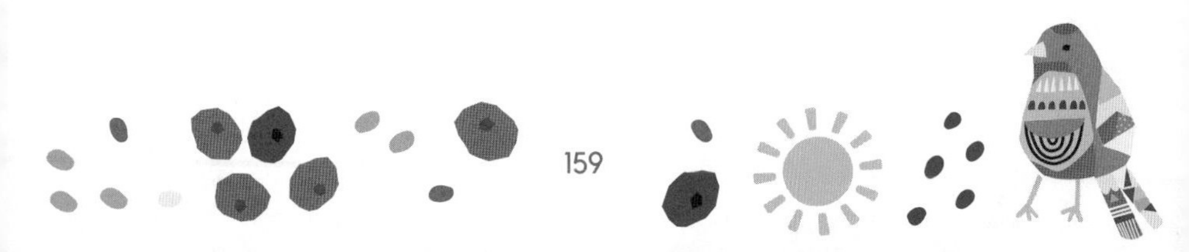

FRIENDS YOU CAN TRUST

It is foolish to belittle one's neighbor; a sensible person keeps quiet. A gossip goes around telling secrets, but those who are trustworthy can keep a confidence.
PROVERBS 11:12–13 NLT

We talked about being trustworthy yesterday. It's a really big deal. Your friends and family want to know that they can trust you. Have you ever been in a group of girls and after someone leaves, some of the girls talk about that person behind their back? That's pretty hurtful. Those girls are not trustworthy because you know that they'll likely talk about you when you leave the room too. Don't be fooled into thinking that they won't do that to you just because they say you are their friend. The Bible says that sensible and trustworthy people don't act like that.

People who love God want the best for you, and they won't put you down when you aren't around. Look for those kinds of friends. Now, think about what kind of person you are: Do your friends trust you? Should they?

Father, please help me to love You and love others well. Help me to be trustworthy, and please forgive me for the times I haven't been. Help me to find trustworthy friends who love You and want to please You with their lives.

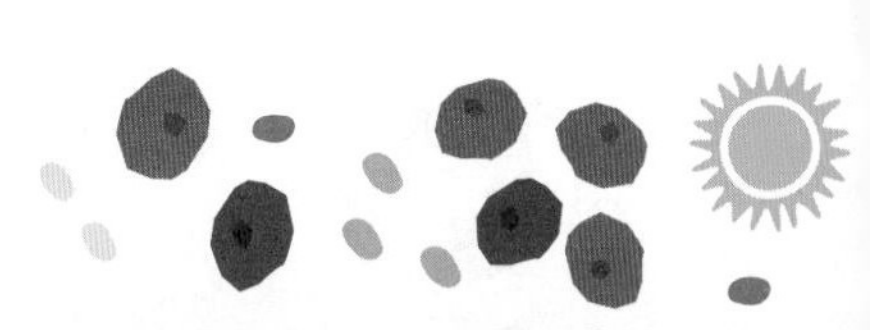

HOPE

May the God of hope fill you with all joy and peace as you trust in him, so that you may overflow with hope by the power of the Holy Spirit.

ROMANS 15:13 NIV

Our God is a God of hope! One of the biblical definitions of hope is to "anticipate with pleasure."

Have you ever been around someone who was super excited for something? Maybe it was a long-awaited dream vacation, and they were counting the days. That person's excitement could barely be contained! Or maybe a friend or relative was planning their wedding. Or a baby was on its way into the world, and the parents could hardly wait to meet their child. That's what hope looks like: anticipating with pleasure something you know is coming. You can't help but get in on the excitement when someone around you is anticipating something wonderful.

As followers of Jesus, we have hope like that. The Holy Spirit can fill us with joy and peace that overflows onto everyone we meet, urging them to participate in our excitement.

If you're missing some of that hope, talk to Jesus about this. Ask for the Holy Spirit to fill you again to overflowing.

Jesus, I want to be filled to the brim with hope, joy, and peace! Let this be contagious in my life.

HOPE FOR SURVIVAL

He spreads snow like a white fleece, he scatters frost like ashes, he broadcasts hail like birdseed—who can survive his winter? Then he gives the command and it all melts; he breathes on winter—suddenly it's spring!

PSALM 147:17–18 MSG

Research has been done on people who have survived atrocious events: being prisoners of war, being lost on a mountain, being kidnapped.

The survivors had one thing in common: hope. If someone has hope, they can hang on. They find strength to hold on a little longer if they believe someone is coming for them.

Hope is a powerful thing. It offers a ray of light when the darkness threatens to overtake us. It helps us take the next step when we feel like we don't have the strength to put one foot in front of the other.

First Timothy 4:10 (NLT) says, "This is why we work hard and continue to struggle, for our hope is in the living God, who is the Savior of all people and particularly of all believers."

Jesus is our living hope. We can keep moving forward because we know His Spirit is alive in us and He's coming for us once again.

Lord Jesus, I've put all my hope and trust in You. I know You're alive in me and You're coming back for me again someday.

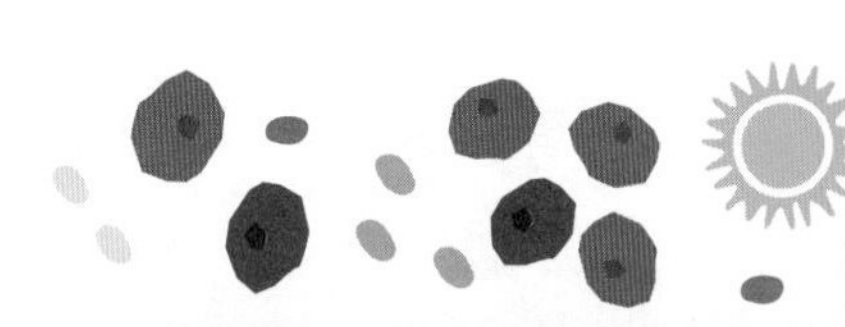

HOPE IN YOUR EYES

"Your eyes are windows into your body. If you open your eyes wide in wonder and belief, your body fills up with light. If you live squinty-eyed in greed and distrust, your body is a musty cellar. If you pull the blinds on your windows, what a dark life you will have!"

MATTHEW 6:22 MSG

You can tell a lot about a person by their eyes. Scientists have studied how the eyes relate to what's going on inside a person. They can tell if a person is lying by what their eyes are doing. Some people have a constant sparkle in their eyes, and they bring joy to any room.

People who love Jesus have a special light in their eyes. Often you can tell people are believers just by the hope and joy that emanates from them. Do you know someone like this? These kinds of people attract others to them. They want to know where the light comes from! God can fill you with that very same kind of hope and joy. Just ask Him!

God of hope, thank You for giving me life. Light up my eyes with wonder and belief. Fill my soul with Your joy and peace. Let others see the difference in me so that I can point them to You.

NEW MERCIES THIS MORNING!

The faithful love of the LORD never ends! His mercies never cease. Great is his faithfulness; his mercies begin afresh each morning.

LAMENTATIONS 3:22–23 NLT

Lucy Maud Montgomery's beloved character Anne Shirley says, "Tomorrow is always fresh with no mistakes in it yet."

Do you know what mercy is? Mercy is when a person in power has the right to punish someone and they choose not to. Grace and mercy often get confused. Grace is when God gives us something that we don't deserve (like forgiveness and special blessings). Mercy is when God chooses not to give us something we do deserve (such as punishment for sin).

God does this because of Jesus taking our punishment on the cross. The Bible tells us that God's mercies are new every morning. So if you feel like you've made a bunch of mistakes this week, talk to God about them. Ask Him to forgive you and give you a pure heart. Then start your day confidently, knowing that our great God forgives you and loves you. God is always ready to give you a fresh start.

Thank You, Father, for a fresh start each day. Even when others hold grudges against me sometimes, You never do. Thank You for giving me hope in a new day. Help me to follow You with my whole heart today.

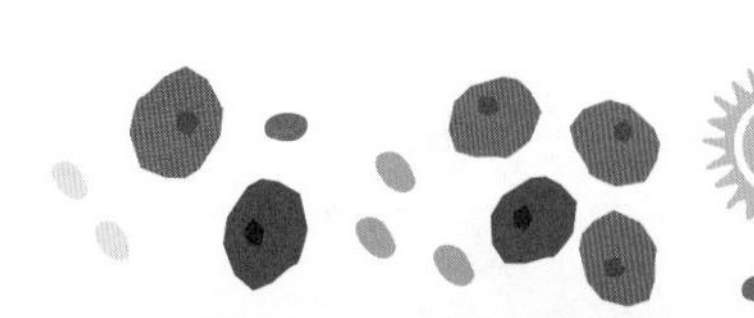

HOPE AND REST

I wait for the LORD, my whole being waits,
and in his word I put my hope.
PSALM 130:5 NIV

Do you feel like you're always in a hurry? Many girls your age run from one activity to the next: school, piano lessons, church, gymnastics, youth group, volleyball, a birthday party—and on and on it goes. Does your life feel like that sometimes?

Having lots of activities can be a fun and exciting way to live, but God wants to make sure we have time to rest too. Too many activities and not enough rest aren't good for your mind, body, or soul.

Remember that God took a rest after He created the world. The Bible says He blessed that day and made it holy (Genesis 2:1–3). Did the God of all creation need a rest? No, of course not. He is God! But He rested as an example for us to follow. God wants us to rest from our work and our activities. He wants us to create space for Him in our lives.

Father, sometimes I'm not very good at resting and creating space for You in my life. Would You please help me with that? Show me how to live a better life—a life that honors Your Word and keeps my body, mind, and soul healthy.

QUIET HOPE

God proves to be good to the man who passionately waits, to the woman who diligently seeks. It's a good thing to quietly hope, quietly hope for help from God. It's a good thing when you're young to stick it out through the hard times.

Lamentations 3:25–27 MSG

It's interesting that *The Message* uses "quietly hope" twice in a row. "It's a good thing to quietly hope, quietly hope for help from God." Have you ever "quietly hoped" for something from God?

When my daughter Jessa broke her leg, we knew it was bad. She damaged her growth plate, and the surgeon was concerned that one of her legs would grow to be longer than the other. He even told us that they might have to go in and break the other leg so that they would be even!

After surgery to fix the break, we did everything the doctors told us to do. All the while, we knew that God was the great Healer. We quietly hoped for Him to fuse the bone back together and heal her leg good as new.

We're still in the waiting period of quiet hope, not knowing how this will all turn out and trusting God to heal.

Lord, we quietly hope for You to help! We trust in Your goodness and great power over our lives.

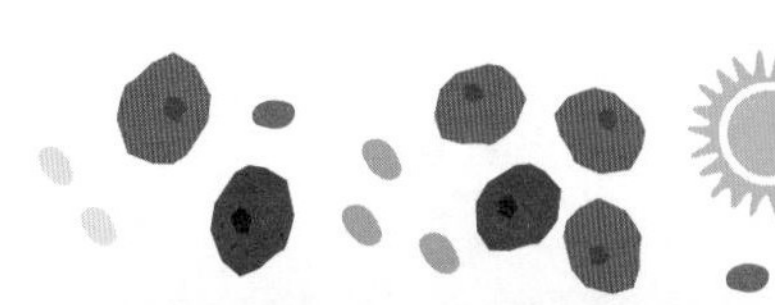

THE HOPE YOU HAVE

In your hearts revere Christ as Lord. Always be prepared to give an answer to everyone who asks you to give the reason for the hope that you have. But do this with gentleness and respect, keeping a clear conscience, so that those who speak maliciously against your good behavior in Christ may be ashamed of their slander.

1 Peter 3:15–16 NIV

If you're living your life to follow Christ, other people are going to wonder about you! If you love God and treat other people with kindness, you're going to get questions about why you do what you do. Are you ready to answer them?

Some people may be unkind and make fun of you for being a Christian. The world seems to be getting more hostile toward Christ followers by the minute! Their words might make you angry. Please pause here! Before you answer them, ask for God's help. He is right there with you, and He sees everything that's happening. He wants you to answer with gentleness and respect, not anger and embarrassment. Many times the reason they're asking is because they are looking for hope too! And they want to know if yours is real.

Father, help me to be gentle and respectful of others when I share my hope and faith in You.

HOPE IN THE SERVANT KING

"Here is my servant whom I have chosen, the one I love, in whom I delight; I will put my Spirit on him, and he will proclaim justice to the nations. . . . In his name the nations will put their hope."
MATTHEW 12:18, 21 NIV

Jesus was all about servant leadership. That means He led His followers by showing them how to love and serve other people. He didn't arrive as a king who would sit on His throne and be served. He came to serve and show love. He even washed His disciples' feet to make His point very clear! He loved them.

People wore sandals everywhere in Jesus' day. Their feet were dirty, and when entering a home, it was the servant's job to wash the guests' feet. Jesus did that Himself. Loving leaders serve their people humbly.

The people in Bible times were expecting their Messiah to come and save them from Roman occupation and persecution with victory and rule over the wicked. They weren't sure what to do with Jesus because He came as a gentle servant, quietly showing the way to lead others to truth and freedom. What kind of leader are you? Ask Jesus to help you lead like He does!

Jesus, show me how to lead others out of love.
Let me point the way to hope in You.

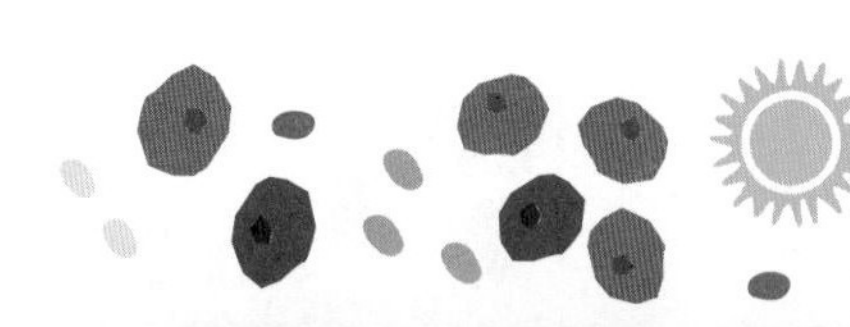

JESUS IS COMING BACK!

Now faith is confidence in what we hope for and assurance about what we do not see.
HEBREWS 11:1 NIV

Seeing Jesus coming on the clouds is the great hope of all believers. Jesus said in Matthew 24:30 (NLV), "They will see the Son of Man coming in the clouds of the sky with power and shining-greatness."

This is what we Christians are patiently waiting for. We're waiting for the day when Jesus comes and makes all things new again, gets rid of all evil in the world forever, wipes away all tears and sadness, and we get to spend eternity with Him.

We were made for another world where Jesus Christ is King forever. That's why some things will always feel wrong and sad here. We were made to live in a sin-free world with Jesus.

It's important to live every day as if Jesus could be returning today, because He could! But until you see Jesus coming in the clouds, keep talking to Jesus and loving others. Is there anything you would do differently if you knew Jesus were coming back today?

Jesus, I'm excited to know You are coming back to make all things right in this dark world! No more sadness and hurting people! Help me live for You patiently as I wait for Your return.

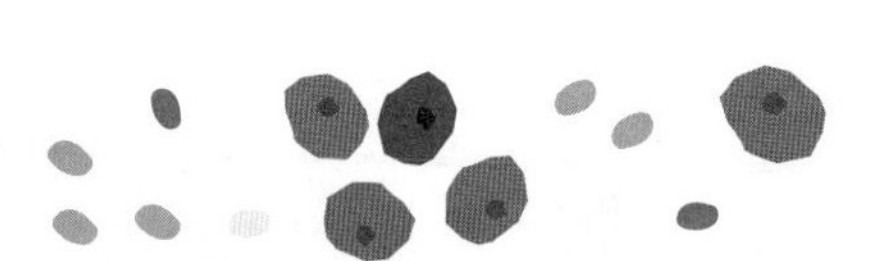

TAKE HOPE!

Jesus stopped and told them to call the blind man. They called to him and said, "Take hope! Stand up, He is calling for you!"
MARK 10:49 NLV

Jesus, His disciples, and a large crowd were all walking together out of the city. But Jesus stopped to pay attention to one blind beggar who was sitting beside the road, calling to Jesus to have mercy on him. Jesus stopped and listened. He called for the blind beggar to come to Him. So the man jumped up and went to Jesus. Jesus healed his eyes, and the man followed Him along the road.

But if we back up a little, in Mark 10:48 (NLV) we read, "Many people spoke sharp words to the blind man telling him not to call out like that. But he spoke all the more. He said, 'Son of David, take pity on me.'"

Jesus had compassion on this poor man as he "took hope" and reached out to Jesus. And Jesus healed him. A wise leader does what God wants him to do, not what the crowd wants him to do.

Jesus, help me to be a wise leader like You. Help me listen to others and have compassion for them no matter what the crowd says.

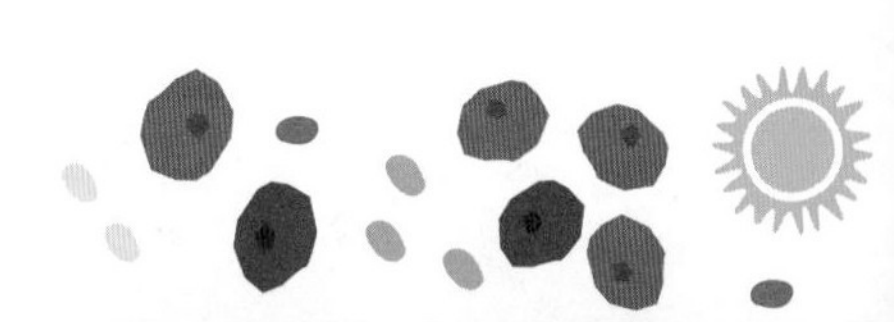

HOPE AND ENCOURAGEMENT

"I have told you these things so you may have peace in Me. In the world you will have much trouble. But take hope! I have power over the world!"
John 16:33 NLV

Life isn't easy. Growing up is hard work. Jesus knows this! He had to grow up too! He wants you to know that He understands everything you are going through. He is there for you, waiting to help you through every situation. Check out this encouragement from His Word:

- "Have I not commanded you? Be strong and courageous. Do not be afraid; do not be discouraged, for the Lord your God will be with you wherever you go." (Joshua 1:9 NIV)
- "For I am the Lord your God who takes hold of your right hand and says to you, Do not fear; I will help you." (Isaiah 41:13 NIV)
- "The Lord is my light and my salvation—whom shall I fear? The Lord is the stronghold of my life—of whom shall I be afraid?" (Psalm 27:1 NIV)
- "You, dear children, are from God and have overcome [the antichrist spirits], because the one who is in you is greater than the one who is in the world." (1 John 4:4 NIV)

Jesus, I'm glad You understand my life! Thanks for giving me hope and encouragement from Your Word!

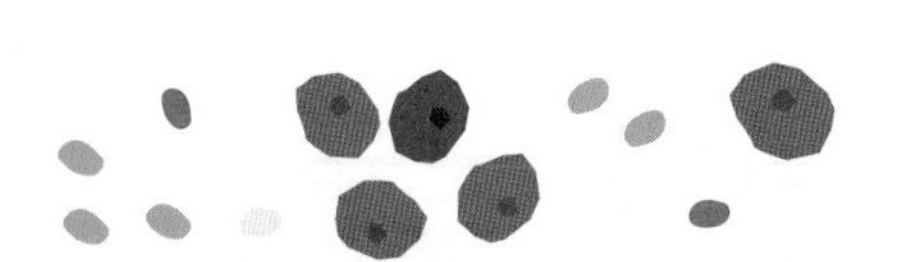

ALL YOUR HOPE

Since God assured us, "I'll never let you down, never walk off and leave you," we can boldly quote, God is there, ready to help; I'm fearless no matter what. Who or what can get to me?
HEBREWS 13:5–6 MSG

God is with you always; He promises never to leave you. And He's the only one who never ever breaks a promise! Numbers 23:19 (NLT) says, "God is not a man, so he does not lie. He is not human, so he does not change his mind. Has he ever spoken and failed to act? Has he ever promised and not carried it through?"

There is great hope and encouragement in these scriptures today. If you've been hurt by someone in the past, it's easy to hang on to that hurt for a while. You may have forgiven the offender, but the hurt still causes you to second guess and have a hard time trusting in the future.

People will fail you. Even the most loving and well-meaning person on the planet can let you down. But Jesus never will. You can put all your hope and trust in Him, letting Him love you and meet all your needs. And then you won't want things from human beings that they weren't designed to give you.

Jesus, I come to You to get all my needs met.
Thank You for loving me so well.

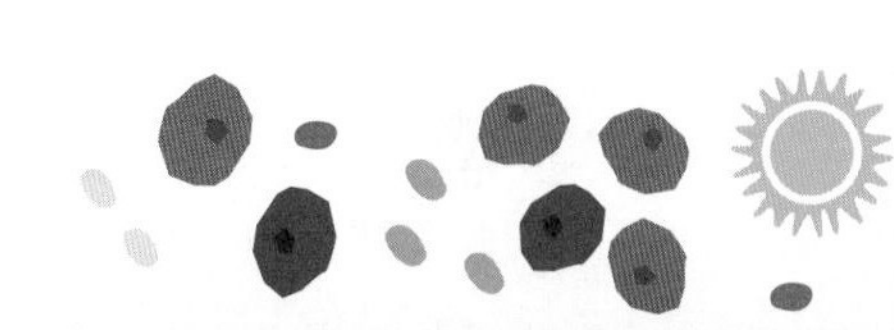

CHRIST IN YOU

"I have made Your name known to them and will make it known. So then the love You have for Me may be in them and I may be in them."
JOHN 17:26 NLV

Jesus was praying for His disciples and for all future believers. That's us! Yes, Jesus prayed to the Father for *you*! Jesus' disciples didn't understand that when He went back to heaven, He would send His Spirit to live in our hearts and still be alive in us. So they didn't want Him to leave. When Jesus was here on earth, He had limits because He was in a human body. He couldn't be everywhere at the same time. Now that He has risen and conquered death, His Spirit can be everywhere at once.

Check it out: "This mystery has been kept in the dark for a long time, but now it's out in the open. God wanted everyone, not just Jews, to know this rich and glorious secret inside and out, regardless of their background, regardless of their religious standing. The mystery in a nutshell is just this: Christ is in you, so therefore you can look forward to sharing in God's glory. It's that simple" (Colossians 1:27 MSG).

Jesus, let Your Spirit come alive inside my heart so I can live for You and with You forever.

DON'T LOSE HOPE

Then Jesus said to them again, "May you have peace. As the Father has sent Me, I also am sending you."
JOHN 20:21 NLV

Jesus has given us all work to do on this earth as we wait for Him to come back. We have gifts and talents to serve Him and share His love with others. And when we've been faithful in the little things, we'll be given bigger things as He continues to send us out as lights to the world.

But humans easily lose interest in a job once they are stuck on a problem or bored with it. You can relate, right? Finishing a job requires faithfulness. Finishing the job *well* requires prayer and dependence on Jesus.

Galatians 5:6 (NIV) tells us, "The only thing that counts is faith expressing itself through love." So if you're feeling tired and weak or bored, remember that Jesus can be your strength. He can help you love like He loved while you get the job done. And that's the only thing that really counts.

Jesus, I ask that You would help me to be faithful in all the tasks that You give me on this earth. Help me not to lose hope when problems come but to finish the job well as I trust in You for help.

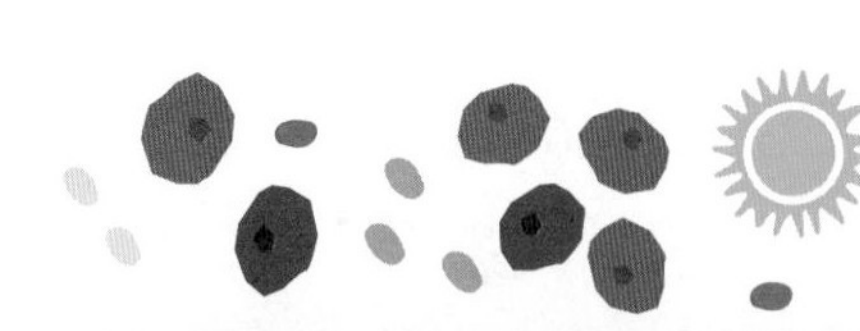

HOPE IN GOD'S WORD

Jesus did many other powerful works in front of His followers. They are not written in this book. But these are written so you may believe that Jesus is the Christ, the Son of God. When you put your trust in Him, you will have life that lasts forever through His name.

John 20:30–31 NLV

Part of trusting Jesus is trusting in the hope and truth of His Word. As believers, we trust that the Bible is the inspired Word of God. Second Timothy 3:16 (NIV) tells us what that means: "All Scripture is God-breathed and is useful for teaching, rebuking, correcting and training in righteousness."

How can we know the Bible is true? Don't be afraid to search out the truth for yourself. Many people have come to know Jesus by trying to prove the Bible wrong! AnswersInGenesis.org says this about the Bible: "It has been confirmed countless times by archaeology and other sciences. It possesses divine insight into the nature of the universe and has made correct predictions about distant future events with perfect accuracy." The Word of God can be trusted.

If you want to know how to live your life for God, if you need wisdom for today and hope for tomorrow, get into God's Word. It will change your life!

Jesus, thank You for the hope and truth I have in Your Word!

HELP FOR THE JOURNEY

Let the morning bring me word of your unfailing love, for I have put my trust in you. Show me the way I should go, for to you I entrust my life. Rescue me from my enemies, LORD, for I hide myself in you. Teach me to do your will, for you are my God; may your good Spirit lead me on level ground.

PSALM 143:8–10 NIV

The psalmist was hoping to wake up in the morning and be reminded of God's love. He wanted hope for the day and help for the journey.

Today's scripture is a great way to start any morning. Let's use it as a prayer guide:

- "Let the morning bring me word of your unfailing love": Good morning, Lord. I'm thankful for this new day and for how much You love me. I put my trust in You!
- "Show me the way I should go": I'm listening for Your voice today, Lord. Help me follow what I hear You say.
- "Rescue me": Protect me from the arrows of the enemy. Hide me from Satan's attacks.
- "Teach me to do Your will": I'm ready to follow You today, Lord.

Praying God's Word is a powerful tool and a good habit to practice!

Lord, You are so good. You offer help and hope for the journey, and I'm thankful!

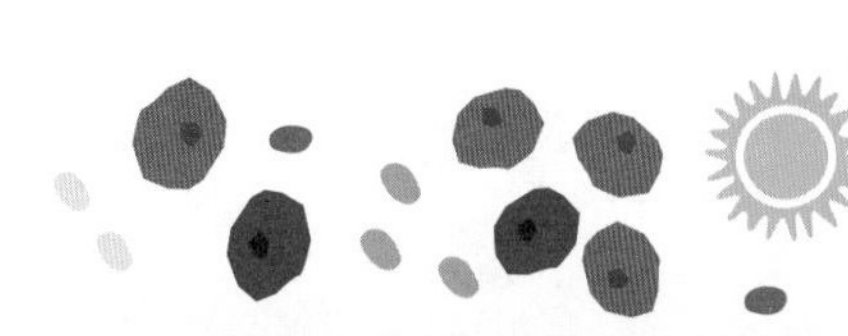

HOPE AND FORGIVENESS

"Therefore I say to you, her sins, which are many, are forgiven, for she loved much; but he who is forgiven little, loves little."
LUKE 7:47 AMP

A sinful woman went into the house of a Pharisee to anoint Jesus' feet with an expensive bottle of oil. The Pharisees were disgusted that Jesus let this sinful woman touch Him. Her sins were many. She was known in the town for her bad choices. But Jesus welcomed her. He forgave her sins and offered her peace.

Like this sinful woman, we've been forgiven much. Jesus took care of all that for us on the cross. He paid for our past, present, and future sins. C. S. Lewis said, "Christ died for men precisely because men are not worth dying for; to make them worth it."

Jesus made us worth dying for. We don't understand it, we don't know why He loves us—but He chooses to. He offers us a completely clear conscience. And as Christ followers, we can live out our short time on earth with joy and hopeful expectation!

Jesus, thank You for Your forgiveness of all my sins. You've given hope to the world, covering every sin. I'm grateful for what You've done for me. Please give me boldness to share that with others who need Your hope and forgiveness.

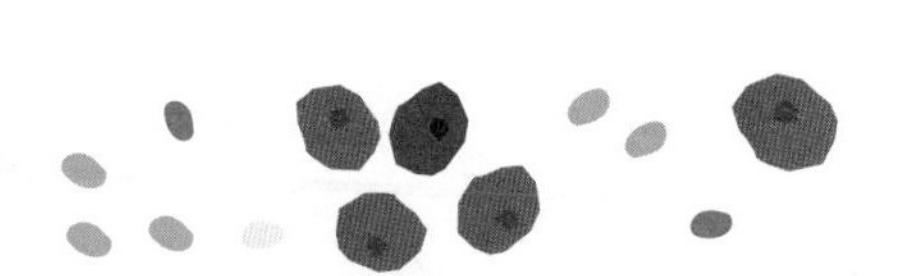

HOPE SINGS

God, the one and only—I'll wait as long as he says. Everything I hope for comes from him, so why not? He's solid rock under my feet, breathing room for my soul, an impregnable castle: I'm set for life.

Psalm 62:5 MSG

Poet Emily Dickinson wrote, "'Hope' is the thing with feathers that perches in the soul, and sings the tune without the words and never stops at all."

Dickinson's words give a picture of the word *hope*. You suddenly see it as a little bird, swinging and singing a lovely tune in your soul. Hope is like that! And it comes from God alone. He's the source of hope (and birds, for that matter!). Psalm 61:8 (MSG) says, "I'll be the poet who sings your glory—and live what I sing every day."

As you open the cage of your heart, hope is free to bring joy and delight to everyone it encounters. Hope sings, and that hope can make a difference in a dark world. As you share Your hope with others, remember that Jesus is the hope of the world.

Live what you believe. Live your song.

Lord Jesus, You are the source of my hope and joy. Help me to live an authentic life, living out what I sing and what I hope for.

A FRIEND OF JESUS

Jesus summoned His twelve disciples and gave them authority and power over unclean spirits, to cast them out, and to heal every kind of disease and every kind of sickness.

MATTHEW 10:1 AMP

Jesus called twelve men to follow Him. He didn't demand that these twelve do exactly what He said. He asked them to follow Him, and He gave them each a choice. They became His disciples and friends. He chose normal, everyday guys—men who probably thought they could never be used by God. Some were fishermen—and one was even a tax collector who was hated by his own people! Jesus gave these regular guys extraordinary power to change the world. Jesus used them to show that He can use anyone.

The same is true today. God offers you the choice to follow Him and become His friend. You may not think that you have any great talents or gifts that God can use. But God can use anything you bring to Him and turn it into something that brings honor to Him and blessing to you. If you are a friend of Jesus, He has great plans for you!

Jesus, I trust Your great plans for me. I bring all that I have to You to use. Thanks for being my Friend.

A HOPELESS SITUATION

Then he walked over to the coffin and touched it, and the bearers stopped. "Young man," he said, "I tell you, get up." Then the dead boy sat up and began to talk! And Jesus gave him back to his mother.

LUKE 7:14–15 NLT

As Jesus was walking among the crowd, He witnessed a desperate situation. A young man was dead, and he was being carried through the town. He was the only son of a widow. Because the main wage earner in the family had died, the widow was probably going to have a lot of financial problems in the future. She was sad and probably scared. What could be done? Her son was already dead. But then Jesus saw her.

Luke 7:13 (NLT) says, "When the Lord saw her, his heart overflowed with compassion. 'Don't cry!' he said." Then He commanded the dead man to get up—and he did!

Jesus can take a completely hopeless situation and turn it around. Whenever you feel like a problem is completely impossible, reach out to Jesus. He can do what He's always done. Trust that He can do the impossible and bring hope to hopeless situations.

Jesus, help me to trust that You can bring hope to any situation. Show me how to share this hope with my friends and family members.

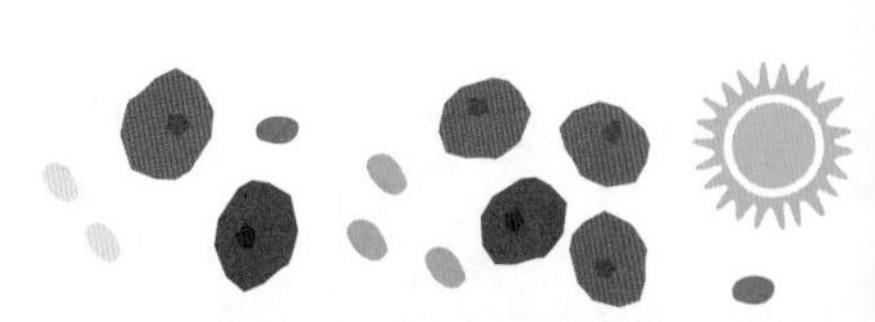

GOOD PLANS AND HOPE

"For I know the plans I have for you," declares the LORD, "plans to prosper you and not to harm you, plans to give you hope and a future."
JEREMIAH 29:11 NIV

Bad days come and go. Life can get weird. You may feel like sticking your head under the covers from time to time. But even when those times come at you, you can be certain that God is still good and still at work in your life, working everything out for your good and for His glory (Romans 8:28).

Even if your own poor choices have caused these circumstances and you feel like there is no hope and no way out, God sees. He is loving and gracious. He welcomes you back into His arms and says, "I'm here. You are not alone. I will never leave you."

God's unfailing love is always at work, redeeming you—even if it doesn't feel like it.

Psalm 13:5–6 (NIV) says, "I trust in your unfailing love; my heart rejoices in your salvation. I will sing the LORD's praise, for he has been good to me."

God has good plans for you, girl. Trust Him!

Thanks for this reminder, Lord. I'm going to trust that You are at work in my life. Thanks for the hope I have in You!

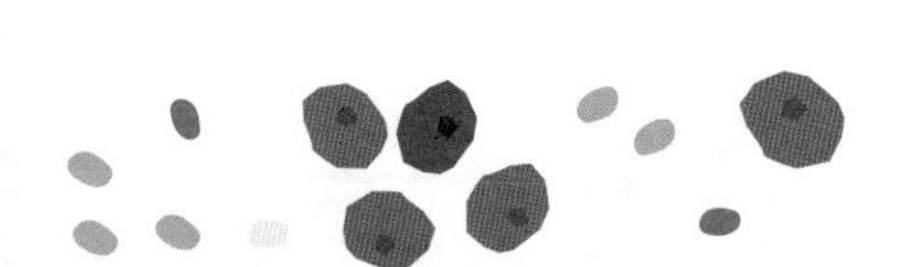

NOAH'S HOPE

Then God said, "I am giving you a sign of my covenant with you and with all living creatures, for all generations to come. I have placed my rainbow in the clouds. It is the sign of my covenant with you and with all the earth."

GENESIS 9:12–13 NLT

Did you know that it took Noah decades to build the ark and get it ready for the great flood? People must have thought he was nuts for building a giant boat on dry land for years and years.

But God gave Noah hope and a job. The Bible says that Noah found favor in God's eyes, so God protected him. Noah obeyed everything God said. And miraculously when the time was near, animals start showing up two by two, as if they had reservations.

It rained for forty days and nights. The earth was completely flooded for 150 days. I imagine that must have been pretty scary for Noah and his family. They were the only family left alive on earth! But they trusted God, and God kept His promise to them.

When it was safe, God called Noah and his family out of the ark and blessed them. They started over with God's promise written in the sky—a rainbow.

Lord, I'm thankful that You gave us a do-over with Noah's family. Help me to love and honor You always.

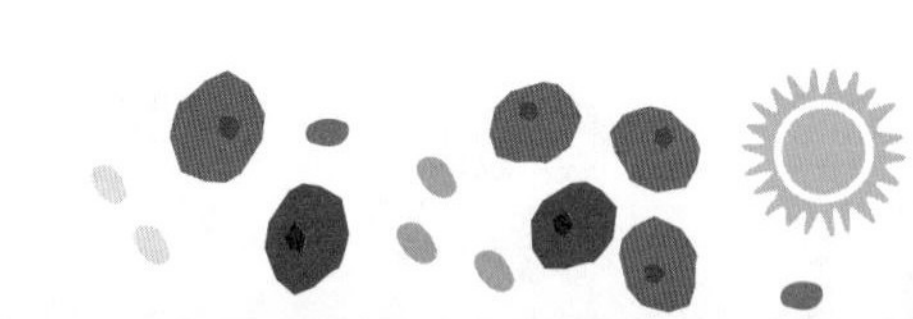

JOSEPH (PART 1)

The Lord was with Joseph, so he succeeded in everything he did as he served in the home of his Egyptian master.

Genesis 39:2 NLT

Joseph's story in the Bible starts in Genesis 37. He came on the scene as a spoiled teenage boy. He knew his father loved him more than all his other brothers. He bragged about special dreams God gave him. That didn't go over well. In fact, it stirred up hatred in the hearts of his brothers. So guess what they did? They sold him!

Now, you might get upset with your siblings a time or two, but would you get so mad that you wanted to sell them?

So Joseph was sold into slavery in Egypt. He probably learned a lot of lessons in humility along the way. But he remembered the dreams God gave him, and that gave him hope. God was with him in Egypt and had a plan and purpose for him there. He found favor in his master's household and was put in charge. Things were about to get a little more difficult first, however. We'll see what happens tomorrow.

Lord, I love hearing about all the ways You've given Your people hope through the ages. I'm thankful I have Your Word to learn from.

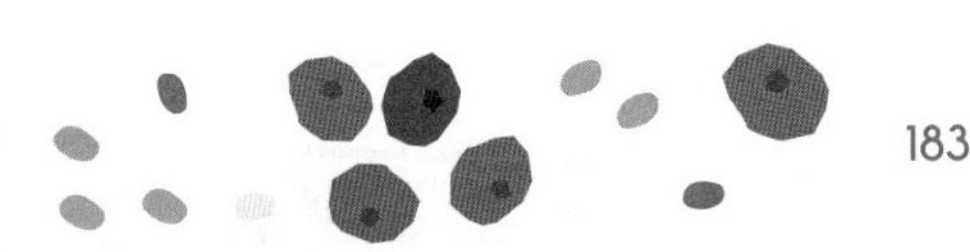

JOSEPH (PART 2)

But the LORD was with Joseph in the prison and showed him his faithful love. And the LORD made Joseph a favorite with the prison warden.
GENESIS 39:21 NLT

Joseph's master, Potiphar, was a wealthy man who trusted Joseph. Genesis 39:5 (NLT) says, "From the day Joseph was put in charge of his master's household and property, the LORD began to bless Potiphar's household for Joseph's sake. All his household affairs ran smoothly, and his crops and livestock flourished."

The problems started when Potiphar's wife decided she wanted to have an affair with Joseph. Joseph refused and told her he would not sin against God in that way. This made her mad. So she set him up! She lied to her husband about Joseph, and Joseph was thrown in jail. The word of a rich woman trumped the word of a Hebrew slave.

But Joseph still trusted that God had a plan for his life. And quickly he found favor with the prison warden. Soon Joseph was in charge of everything at the prison. God was faithful.

There's even more to Joseph's hopeful story. Catch part 3 tomorrow.

Wow, Lord. Joseph's story is dramatic! And here I thought my challenges were rough. I'm thankful to know that You're with me, just like You were with Joseph in all his struggles.

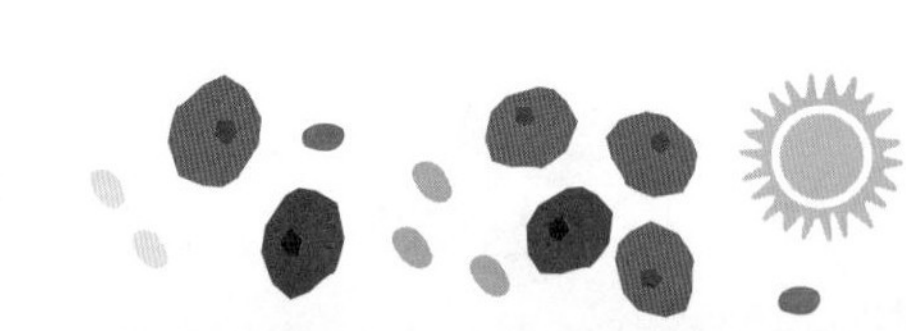

JOSEPH (PART 3)

So Pharaoh asked his officials, "Can we find anyone else like this man so obviously filled with the spirit of God?" Then Pharaoh said to Joseph, "Since God has revealed the meaning of the dreams to you, clearly no one else is as intelligent or wise as you are. You will be in charge of my court, and all my people will take orders from you. Only I, sitting on my throne, will have a rank higher than yours."

GENESIS 41:38–40 NLT

Joseph asked God to help him interpret Pharaoh's dreams, and He did. This made Pharaoh very happy. So Joseph, a Hebrew who was sold into slavery by his own brothers, was put in charge of all of Egypt!

Just as Pharaoh's dreams predicted, the crops were good for seven years. So Joseph stored crops and grain. Then, also as predicted, seven years of famine came. But the Egyptians had plenty of food because of all of Joseph's preparation. The surrounding areas, however, did not. Including the land of Joseph's family and brothers.

God was with Joseph during all of the difficult times he endured. God placed him exactly where He wanted him.

Even if a situation seems impossible, remember God is at work behind the scenes.

Joseph's story gives me hope, Lord. Even in tragic circumstances, You were working in his life.

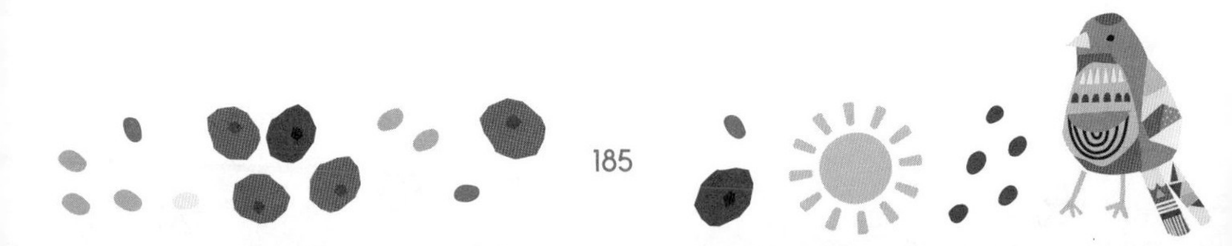

JOSEPH (FINALE)

"Please, come closer," [Joseph] said to [his brothers]. So they came closer. And he said again, "I am Joseph, your brother, whom you sold into slavery in Egypt. But don't be upset, and don't be angry with yourselves for selling me to this place. It was God who sent me here ahead of you to preserve your lives."
GENESIS 45:4–5 NLT

People were starving during the famine. Seven years was too long to go without a good crop. Joseph's father, who had no idea that Joseph was still alive, heard that Egypt had food. He sent his sons to go and buy some.

And that's when Joseph saw his brothers again for the first time since they sold him as a slave. He had grown into a man during that time, and his brothers didn't recognize him. But after a series of events, Joseph finally revealed himself to his brothers. He forgave them completely and gave them everything they needed.

Joseph's dramatic story started when he was a teenager who was given dreams and hope from God. That hope kept him going through all the trials he faced. And looking at his brothers after all that time, he saw God's hand in everything.

Lord, help me to forgive as Joseph did and hold on to hope as I grow up.

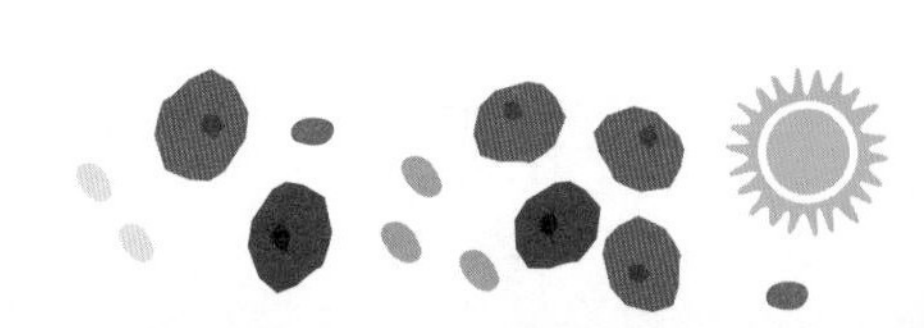

TIME FOR A CELEBRATION

Praise the LORD, for the LORD is good; celebrate his lovely name with music.
PSALM 135:3 NLT

Has God been good to you? Do you have a lot to be thankful for? Let's praise Him for that. Turn up the praise music and dance your way through this morning. Thank God for all He's done for you! Use these scriptures as your guide:

- "I will thank the LORD because he is just; I will sing praise to the name of the LORD Most High." (Psalm 7:17 NLT)
- "Sing joyfully to the LORD, you righteous; it is fitting for the upright to praise him." (Psalm 33:1 NIV)
- "I will be filled with joy because of you. I will sing praises to your name, O Most High." (Psalm 9:2 NLT)
- "Sing the praises of the LORD, you his faithful people; praise his holy name." (Psalm 30:4 NIV)
- "My tongue will proclaim your righteousness, your praises all day long." (Psalm 35:28 NIV)
- "Sing praises to God, sing praises; sing praises to our King, sing praises!" (Psalm 47:6 NLT)
- "For God is the King over all the earth. Praise him with a psalm." (Psalm 47:7 NLT)

Lord, You give me hope when I'm feeling lost. You have been so good to me! You are loving and kind. I'm glad I'm Your child!

HOPE FOR THE HOPELESS

[Jesus] went throughout all Galilee, teaching in their synagogues and preaching the good news (gospel) of the kingdom, and healing every kind of disease and every kind of sickness among the people [demonstrating and revealing that He was indeed the promised Messiah].

Matthew 4:23 AMP

Jesus came to bring hope to hopeless people. He came to bring freedom and joy to people who have never known happiness. He healed sickness, He raised people from the dead, He freed people from all their sin and shame. He was and is the living hope. As a follower of Jesus, you carry that hope inside you.

You're going to run into a lot of people in your lifetime who need to know there is hope. You have it. You know where it comes from.

First Peter 1:3–5 (NIV) says, "Praise be to the God and Father of our Lord Jesus Christ! In his great mercy he has given us new birth into a living hope through the resurrection of Jesus Christ from the dead, and into an inheritance that can never perish, spoil or fade. This inheritance is kept in heaven for you."

That's the hope! Share it with someone today.

Jesus, You are my living hope. Burst up and out of me, overflowing to others who need Your hope.

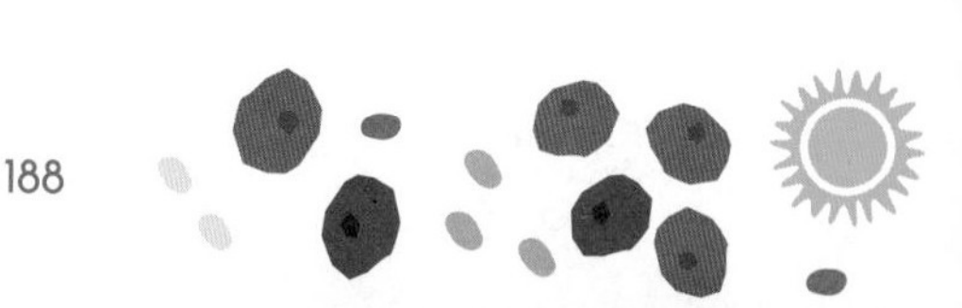

INDEX

Old Testament

New Testament